WordShop

A Vocabulary Tool Kit

Level F

JAMESTOWN PUBLISHERS

a division of NTC/Contemporary Publishing Group
Lincolnwood, Illinois USA

Project Development: Cottage Communications
Cover Design: Ophelia M. Chambliss
Cover Illustration: Rob Colvin

Acknowledgments

The pronunciation key used in the dictionary has been reprinted by permission from the American Heritage Dictionary of the English Language, 3d ed., © 1992 by Houghton Mifflin Company.

ISBN: 0-89061-924-7 (Pupil's Edition)
ISBN: 0-89061-935-2 (Annotated Teacher's Edition)

Published by Jamestown Publishers,
a division of NTC/Contemporary Publishing Group, Inc.,
4255 West Touhy Avenue
Lincolnwood (Chicago), Illinois 60646-1975, U.S.A.

© 1998 NTC/Contemporary Publishing Group, Inc.
All rights reserved. No part of this book may be reproduced, stored in a retrieval system, or transmitted in any form or by any means, electronic, mechanical, photocopying, recording, or otherwise, without prior permission of the publisher.

Manufactured in the United States of America.

5 6 7 8 9 10 11 12 113 09 08 07 06 05

Contents

Lesson 1
Context Clues: The Humanities
Robin Hood, Prince of Thieves 1
Mastering Meaning 4

Lesson 2
Vocabulary of Activity and Action 5
Spelling and Meaning 8

Lesson 3
The Roots *-frac-* and *-rupt-* 9
Cultural Literacy Note 12

Assessment, Lessons 1–3 13

Lesson 4
Context Clues: Social Studies
The Pony Express 15
Mastering Meaning 18

Lesson 5
Vocabulary of Saving and Spending 19
Bonus Words 22

Lesson 6
The Roots *-vis-* and *-audi-* 23
Test-Taking Strategies 26

Assessment, Lessons 4–6 27

Lesson 7
Context Clues: The Sciences
Meteors 29
Mastering Meaning 32

Lesson 8
Vocabulary of Quantity and Amount 33
Using the Dictionary 36

Lesson 9
The Prefix *re-* 37
Our Living Language 40

Assessment, Lessons 7–9 41

Lesson 10
Context Clues: The Humanities
Aesop's Fables 43
Mastering Meaning 46

Lesson 11
Vocabulary of Geometry 47
Cultural Literacy Note 50

Lesson 12
The Prefixes *ex-* and *extra-* 51
Test-Taking Strategies 54
Assessment, Lessons 10–12 55

Lesson 13
Context Clues: Social Studies
The Maya 57
Mastering Meaning 60

Lesson 14
Confusing Pairs 61
Our Living Language 64

Lesson 15
The Prefix *un-* 65
Bonus Words 68
Assessment, Lessons 13–15 69

Lesson 16
Context Clues: The Sciences
The Rescue of the Peregrine Falcon 71
Mastering Meaning 74

Lesson 17
Vocabulary of Geography 75
Using the Dictionary 78

Lesson 18
The Prefixes *be-* and *mal-* 79
Test-Taking Strategies 82
Assessment, Lessons 16–18 83

Lesson 19
Context Clues: The Humanities
Pecos Bill: An American Tall Tale 85
Mastering Meaning 88

Lesson 20
Vocabulary of Food 89
Cultural Literacy Note 92

Lesson 21
The Suffix *-logy* 93
Bonus Words 96

Assessment, Lessons 19–21 97

Lesson 22
Context Clues: Social Studies
The Church and the State 99
Mastering Meaning 102

Lesson 23
Vocabulary of Society 103
Bonus Words 106

Lesson 24
The "Big" and "Small" Affixes 107
Test-Taking Strategies 110

Assessment, Lessons 22–24 111

Lesson 25
Context Clues: The Sciences
Earthquake! 113
Mastering Meaning 116

Lesson 26
Vocabulary from Spanish 117
Spelling and Meaning 120

Lesson 27
The Roots *-mit-* and *-man-* 121
Our Living Language 124

Assessment, Lessons 25–27 125

Lesson 28
Context Clues: The Humanities
The Arthurian Legend 127
Mastering Meaning 130

Lesson 29
Vocabulary of the Sea 131
Using the Dictionary 134

Lesson 30
Related Words 135
✓ *Test-Taking Skills* 138
   Assessment, Lessons 28–30 139

Lesson 31
Context Clues: Social Studies
The 19th Amendment 141
Mastering Meaning 144

Lesson 32
Vocabulary from French 145
Bonus Words 148

Lesson 33
The Roots -*pen*- and -*port*- 149
Bonus Words 152
   Assessment, Lessons 31–33 153

Lesson 34
Context Clues: The Sciences
The Rocket's Red Glare 155
Mastering Meaning 158

Lesson 35
Vocabulary of Literature 159
Our Living Language 162

Lesson 36
The Root -*ject*- 163
✓ *Test-Taking Strategies* 166
   Assessment, Lessons 34–36 167

Dictionary 169
Standardized Test Practice 185
Alphabetical Word List 201

Context Clues: The Humanities

Name _____

Robin Hood, Prince of Thieves

Possibly as early as the 12th century, traveling minstrels began singing ballads in praise of the **exploits** of a thief named Robin Hood. His skill in archery, his free and easy lifestyle in Sherwood Forest, and, perhaps most of all, his ability to outwit the Sheriff
5 of Nottingham **endeared** him to the common people. In ballad after ballad, Robin Hood was **consistently** pictured as one who stole only from the rich and shared the **spoils** of his actions with the poor. Even though the legends **portray** him as the enemy of the nobility, Robin Hood possessed an **unflagging** loyalty to
10 his king, Richard the Lion-Hearted. This feeling was shared by many people at the time.

As the stories of this remarkable champion of the people increased in number, so did the size of his colorful band of thieves. A huge hulk of a man called Little John became Robin's most
15 trusted follower. Alan-a-Dale, a minstrel, entertained the group around the evening campfire. The fat and **jocular** Friar Tuck kept everyone amused. In later ballads, Robin acquired a sweetheart, Maid Marian. This story included all the traditional romantic qualities—danger, secret meetings, disguises, and the **ultimate**
20 triumph of true love.

Was Robin Hood a living, breathing human being or merely the **figment** of some balladeer's imagination? Those who claim him to be real offer an interesting and believable **scenario**. The laws protecting the king's forests and deer were quite strict in
25 12th century England. Perhaps a hunter accidentally killed one of the king's deer. As a wanted man, he may have gone into hiding in the deepest part of the forest. There he might have been joined by sympathetic supporters.

Apart from the ballads, however, firm evidence of Robin Hood's
30 existence is hard to find. No scholar or historian of the time mentions him. The events described in the various stories simply could not have happened in the course of one lifetime. Even so, the romantic picture of the Prince of Thieves endures in modern poems, operas, and movies. Robin Hood clearly lives on in legend.

Words
- consistent
- endear
- exploits
- figment
- jocular
- portray
- scenario
- spoils
- ultimate
- unflagging

Unlocking Meaning

Each word in this lesson's word list appears in dark type in the selection you just read. Think about how the vocabulary word is used in the selection; then write the letter for the best answer to each question.

1. An *exploit* (line 2) is a(n) _____.
   (A) sudden burst of energy (B) heroic act
   (C) written account of one's life (D) open field

   1. _____

2. If you *endear* (line 5) yourself to someone, you _____.
   (A) make him or her your enemy (B) betray his or her secrets
   (C) cause him or her to think lovingly of you (D) pay no attention to him or her

   2. _____

3. *Consistently* in line 6 means _____.
   (A) seldom (B) painfully
   (C) angrily (D) without change or difference

   3. _____

4. The *spoils* (line 7) of one's actions are the _____.
   (A) damages they cause (B) stories and songs they create
   (C) benefits they bring (D) honors they are awarded

   4. _____

5. Another word for *portray* (line 8) is _____.
   (A) betray (B) mislead
   (C) hide (D) describe

   5. _____

6. Another word for *unflagging* (line 9) is _____.
   (A) untiring (B) foolish
   (C) doubtful (D) weakening

   6. _____

7. A *jocular* (line 16) person tends to _____.
   (A) remain silent (B) disappear without explanation
   (C) start arguments (D) tell jokes

   7. _____

8. The word *ultimate* in line 19 could best be replaced with _____.
   (A) first (B) final
   (C) temporary (D) senseless

   8. _____

9. A *figment* (line 22) is _____.
   (A) a written symbol or sign (B) something made up
   (C) a type of fruit (D) a musical instrument

   9. _____

10. A *scenario* (line 23) can best be described as a _____.
    (A) picture of a landscape (B) verse from a song
    (C) series of events (D) break in a wall

    10. _____

2   Context Clues: The Humanities

Name _____

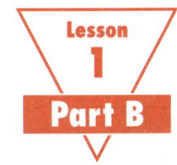

Applying Meaning

Decide which word in parentheses best completes the sentence. Then write the sentence, adding the missing word.

1. The attorney described the _____ leading to the arrest of the accused bank robber. (figment; scenario)

   _____
   _____
   _____

2. Stories of Davy Crockett's _____ seemed to increase in number and importance after he died at the Alamo. (exploits; spoils)

   _____
   _____
   _____

3. The soldiers' _____ devotion to their country and their commander sustained them at Valley Forge. (endearing; unflagging)

   _____
   _____
   _____

4. Her work with the poorest of the poor _____ Mother Teresa to millions throughout the world. (exploited; endeared)

   _____
   _____
   _____

5. One of the _____ of winning an elective office is being provided a car and driver. (figments; spoils)

   _____
   _____
   _____

Each question below contains at least one vocabulary word from this lesson. Answer each question "yes" or "no" in the space provided.

6. Is the branch of a fig tree referred to as a *figment*? 6. _____

7. Do employers want workers who *consistently* arrive on time for work? 7. _____

8. Could an army lose several battles, yet *ultimately* win the war?   8. _____

9. Did Benedict Arnold *portray* his country during the Revolutionary War?   9. _____

10. Is an old, broken-down car sometimes called a *jocular*?   10. _____

For each question you answered "no," write a sentence explaining your answer.

_____
_____
_____
_____
_____
_____
_____
_____

Mastering Meaning

In medieval times, wealth was usually the lucky result of one's noble birth rather than of hard work. It is not surprising, then, that a figure like Robin Hood, who supposedly took from the rich and gave to the poor, would be popular with working-class people. In a free, democratic society, however, such qualities might be less acceptable. Write an essay of at least three paragraphs explaining why a modern day Robin Hood should or should not be considered a hero.

Context Clues: The Humanities

Vocabulary of Activity and Action

Lesson 2 Part A

Name _____

How do you act when the alarm goes off on Monday morning? Do you act differently at a football game? Is there a difference between the way you walk to the dentist and the way you go to movies? Your mood and the situation often determine how you act. The English language has numerous words to describe this endless variety of actions. In this lesson you will study 10 such words.

Words

- agile
- bustle
- dawdle
- diligent
- energetic
- industrious
- negligent
- nimble
- slothful
- sprightly

Unlocking Meaning

Read the sentences or short passages below. Write the letter for the correct definition of the italicized vocabulary word.

1. Using swift, *agile* movements, the quarterback escaped several tacklers until he found a receiver and completed the touchdown pass.
   - (A) slow and methodical
   - (B) unfamiliar
   - (C) circular
   - (D) quick and easy

2. As soon as the race car came to a stop, the pit crew began to *bustle* about, changing the tires, cleaning the windshield, and filling the tank.
   - (A) move busily
   - (B) sneak carefully
   - (C) walk casually
   - (D) remain in one place

3. Juanita *dawdled* all weekend, so she found herself doing her homework at midnight on Sunday.
   - (A) worked hard
   - (B) wasted time
   - (C) moved about constantly
   - (D) studied

4. It took a *diligent* search of the forest and the surrounding lakes, but after several weeks the detectives found the missing coins.
   - (A) determined and careful
   - (B) brief and casual
   - (C) occasional
   - (D) playful

5. Even though the play was presented four times in two days, the actor gave an *energetic* performance that thrilled the audience.
   - (A) weak and feeble
   - (B) surprising
   - (C) powerful
   - (D) unhurried

1. _____

2. _____

3. _____

4. _____

5. _____

6. The parade is only three days away. If the class is to complete its float in time, it will need a group of *industrious* students.
   (A) easygoing (B) stubborn
   (C) emotional (D) hard working and tireless

6. _____

7. Phil forgot to test the lights before the performance. This one *negligent* act ruined one of the best scenes in the play.
   (A) brilliant (B) carefully planned
   (C) thoughtless (D) understandable

7. _____

8. Practicing the scales on a piano does not make beautiful music. It does, however, develop the *nimble* fingers a piano player needs to perform difficult pieces.
   (A) awkward (B) quick moving
   (C) lazy (D) quiet

8. _____

9. It was noon, and Jake still sat around in his robe and slippers while we got the house ready for our guests. His *slothful* behavior was beginning to get on everyone's nerves.
   (A) amusing (B) lazy
   (C) simple (D) gradually increasing

9. _____

10. It comes as no surprise that Marta was made captain of the cheerleading squad. Her *sprightly* behavior and team loyalty are truly inspiring.
    (A) brisk and spirited (B) motionless
    (C) dull (D) foolish

10. _____

6 **Vocabulary of Activity and Action**

Name _____

Lesson 2 — Part B

Applying Meaning

Decide which word in parentheses best completes the sentence. Then write the sentence, adding the missing word.

1. If we had not _____ all afternoon at the mall, we wouldn't have been late for dinner. (bustled; dawdled)

   _____
   _____
   _____

2. Seeing the dog dashing toward it, the squirrel _____ scampered up the tree to safety. (nimbly; slothfully)

   _____
   _____
   _____

3. Critics raved about the ballerina's _____ movements. (agile; diligent)

   _____
   _____
   _____

4. The sergeant made it clear to the new recruits that there was no place for a _____ soldier in an effective army. (diligent; slothful)

   _____
   _____
   _____

5. I try to avoid last-minute Christmas shopping. I can't stand the _____ of such frantic crowds. (bustle; dawdle)

   _____
   _____
   _____

Follow the directions below to write a sentence using a vocabulary word.

6. Use any form of the word *negligent* in a sentence about an accident.

   _____
   _____
   _____

Vocabulary of Activity and Action

7. Use *sprightly* in a sentence about a favorite classmate.
_____
_____
_____

8. Use any form of the word *diligent* in a sentence about doing homework.
_____
_____
_____

9. Use *industrious* in a sentence about something from American history.
_____
_____
_____

10. Use any form of the word *energetic* in a sentence about a famous individual.
_____
_____
_____

Spelling and Meaning

Changing final *y* to *i*

city-cities   study-studied   early-earlier   happy-happiest

If a word ends with a consonant and *y*, change the *y* to *i* before adding *-es*, *-ed*, *-er*, or *-est*.

Combine these words and endings.

1. angry + er = _____
2. heavy + est = _____
3. empty + ed = _____
4. category + es = _____
5. happy + er = _____
6. berry + es = _____

The Roots -frac- and -rupt-

Lesson 3 Part A

Name _____

Latin has two words meaning "to break." One is *rumpere*. The past participle form of this verb is *rotta*. You see this root in English words like *corrupt* and *rupture*, which have kept part of the original Latin meaning. The other Latin word for "to break" is *frangere*. It appears in several forms in words like *fragile*, *frail*, and *fracture*.

Root	Meaning	English Word
-rupt-	broken	rupture
-frag-	broken	fragile

Unlocking Meaning

A vocabulary word appears in italics in each sentence or short passage below. Find the root in the vocabulary word and think about how the word is used in the passage. Then write a definition for the vocabulary word. Compare your definition with the one in the dictionary at the back of the book.

Words
- bankrupt
- corrupt
- disrupt
- eruption
- fracture
- fragile
- fragment
- frail
- infringe
- rupture

1. Television caused some movie theaters to become *bankrupt*, but most managed to survive and make even more money.

   _____
   _____
   _____

2. The candidate vowed to put an end to the bribery and waste in the state's *corrupt* system for hiring state workers.

   _____
   _____
   _____

3. The demonstrators tried to *disrupt* the meeting by shouting at the speaker and carrying a large banner down the aisle.

   _____
   _____
   _____

4. Visitors tried to gather near the geyser to view its hourly *eruption*, but the park ranger made them keep back to avoid injury from its hot steam.

5. The X-ray showed I suffered a *fracture* in my left arm, but the cast should help the bone grow together after about six weeks.

6. The shopkeeper kept the *fragile* antique vase in a locked case. The slightest bump could cause it to shatter.

7. Using just a few *fragments* of the ancient pottery, the museum was able to create a drawing showing what the entire object looked like.

8. After years of confinement and little food, the prisoners of war were so *frail* they had to be carried to the waiting ambulances.

9. The lawyer argued that a tax on newspapers and magazines would *infringe* on the freedom of the press.

10. The cold temperature caused our water pipes to freeze. If they don't thaw soon, the ice will *rupture* them and damage the house.

Name _____

Lesson 3 Part B

Applying Meaning

Decide which word in parentheses best completes the sentence. Then write the sentence, adding the missing word.

1. The flight engineer grounded the plane after he discovered several _____ in the framework of the wings. (eruptions; fractures)

   _____
   _____
   _____

2. The terrorist attack was intended to _____ the peace negotiations between the two nations. (corrupt; disrupt)

   _____
   _____
   _____

3. The _____ lamps and glasses were packed last. (fragile; frail)

   _____
   _____
   _____

4. The teacher felt that one misbehaving student _____ on the rights of students who were trying to study. (infringed; ruptured)

   _____
   _____
   _____

5. The surgeon hurried to repair the weakened artery before it could _____ and endanger the patient's life. (infringe; rupture)

   _____
   _____
   _____

Follow the directions below to write a sentence using a vocabulary word.

6. Use any form of the word *frail* in a sentence about an animal.

   _____
   _____
   _____

The Roots -frac- and -rupt-

7. Write a sentence about credit cards. Use any form of the word *bankrupt*.

   _____
   _____
   _____

8. Use any form of the word *fragment* in a sentence about evidence in a trial.

   _____
   _____
   _____

9. Describe an event in nature. Use any form of the word *eruption*.

   _____
   _____
   _____

10. Describe a real or imaginary person or situation using any form of the word *corrupt*.

    _____
    _____
    _____

Cultural Literacy Note

Frankenstein

After a night of telling ghost stories with friends, Mary Wollstonecraft Shelley, a young woman of 19, imagined and wrote the familiar horror story *Frankenstein*. The term *Frankenstein* has taken on a life of its own. It was originally the name of the mad scientist who created the monster from parts of dead bodies. Almost immediately, however, the name Frankenstein came to refer to the monster he created. Now the term is used to describe anything that goes out of control and destroys its creator. Some people feel that modern scientists created Frankensteins with such inventions as nuclear power and the atomic bomb.

Write an Essay: Think of an invention or agency that you feel qualifies as a Frankenstein. Explain your reasoning in a short essay.

12 The Roots -frac- and -rupt-

Assessment

Lessons 1-3

Name _____

How well do you remember the words you studied in Lessons 1–3? Take the following test covering the words from the last three lessons.

Part 1 Antonyms

Each question below includes a word in capital letters, followed by four words or phrases. Choose the word or phrase that is most nearly <u>opposite</u> in meaning to the word in capital letters. Consider all choices before deciding on your answer. Write the letter for your answer on the line provided.

Sample

| S. SLOW | (A) lazy | (B) simple | S. ___C___ |
| | (C) fast | (D) common | |

1. CONSISTENT	(A) changeable	(B) thoughtless	1. _____
	(C) frequent	(D) uncommon	
2. BANKRUPT	(A) changeable	(B) thoughtless	2. _____
	(C) frequent	(D) wealthy	
3. ENERGETIC	(A) quick	(B) hostile	3. _____
	(C) weak	(D) emotional	
4. ENDEAR	(A) make useful	(B) hostile	4. _____
	(C) entrust	(D) turn away	
5. SLOTHFUL	(A) neat	(B) lively	5. _____
	(C) creative	(D) smart	
6. FRAGILE	(A) delicate	(B) colorful	6. _____
	(C) costly	(D) rugged	
7. AGILE	(A) clumsy	(B) flexible	7. _____
	(C) gentle	(D) calm	
8. JOCULAR	(A) serious	(B) entertaining	8. _____
	(C) learned	(D) blunt	
9. CORRUPT	(A) common	(B) clever	9. _____
	(C) mean	(D) honest	
10. INDUSTRIOUS	(A) factory made	(B) advanced	10. _____
	(C) idle	(D) rewarding	

Assessment 13

11. FRAIL   (A) thin   (B) hardy   11. _____
                      (C) limber   (D) pretty

12. NEGLIGENT   (A) careful   (B) stupid   12. _____
                      (C) kind   (D) unlawful

13. SPRIGHTLY   (A) sluggish   (B) young   13. _____
                      (C) romantic   (D) cute

14. NIMBLE   (A) bouncy   (B) silly   14. _____
                      (C) curious   (D) slow

15. DILIGENT   (A) timely   (B) lazy   15. _____
                      (C) organized   (D) bright

Part 2 Matching Words and Meanings

Match the definition in Column B with the word in Column A. Write the letter of the correct definition on the line provided.

Column A	Column B	
16. spoils	a. piece	16. _____
17. infringe	b. sudden burst	17. _____
18. disrupt	c. most desired	18. _____
19. ultimate	d. chain of events	19. _____
20. exploits	e. crack	20. _____
21. fragment	f. deeds	21. _____
22. eruption	g. violate	22. _____
23. portray	h. benefits	23. _____
24. fracture	i. represent	24. _____
25. scenario	j. interfere with	25. _____

14 Assessment

Context Clues: Social Studies

Name _____

The Pony Express

Until the early 1800s, most Americans **resided** on the East Coast. As the population of eastern cities swelled, many Americans began moving westward to settle the frontier. The West became even more **enticing** when gold was discovered at Sutter's Mill in California in January of 1848. **Prodded** by a **craving** for wealth and riches, thousands of Americans settled in this promising territory.

In addition to attracting miners and fortune hunters, the gold rush also **lured** merchants, craftspersons, and farmers to the West. These new Californians needed a way to **correspond** with family, friends, and associates who remained in the East. In other words, they needed a fast, reliable method of mail delivery between the East and the West. At the time, mail was sent across the country by stagecoach. These coaches **lumbered** slowly over rough trails and were at the mercy of the weather and bandits. The shortcomings of the stagecoach led to the Pony Express, an experiment in rapid mail delivery between Missouri and California. Hoping to win a profitable government contract for cross-country mail delivery, the freighting and express firm of Russell, Majors, and Waddell vowed to carry letters almost 2,000 miles in less than 10 days.

William Hepburn Russell planned a relay system of riders on horseback. To provide fresh horses for the riders, the company established more than 100 stations **approximately** 15 miles apart along a route through Nebraska, Wyoming, and Nevada. Each rider rode about 75 miles of the total route. The Pony Express eventually required nearly 100 hundred riders and more than 400 horses.

The service was **inaugurated** on April 3, 1860. The riders made the journey all year, even during the difficult winter months. Even though the trip was hazardous, only one mail delivery was ever lost.

By late 1861, Russell, Majors, and Waddell had suffered serious money problems. The speed and ease of the telegraph presented **overwhelming** competition to the Pony Express. When overland telegraph connections were completed in October of 1861, Pony Express service was discontinued. This celebrated effort to deliver the mail lasted less than 18 months.

Words

approximate
correspond
crave
enticing
inaugurate
lumber
lure
overwhelming
prod
reside

Unlocking Meaning

Each word in this lesson's word list appears in dark type in the selection you just read. Think about how the vocabulary word is used in the selection; then write the letter for the best answer to each question.

1. To *reside* (line 1) is to _____.
   (A) take flight
   (B) lie beneath the surface
   (C) live in or at a place
   (D) dislike strongly

   1. _____

2. If something is *enticing,* (line 4) it is _____.
   (A) tempting or attractive
   (B) filled with sorrow
   (C) giving off heat
   (D) unfit to be lived in

   2. _____

3. Which word or words could best replace *prodded* in line 5?
   (A) pursued
   (B) completely destroyed
   (C) amused
   (D) urged on

   3. _____

4. A *craving* (line 5) is a(n) _____.
   (A) lengthy conversation
   (B) intense desire
   (C) memory
   (D) dislike

   4. _____

5. To *lure* (line 8) is to _____.
   (A) tempt or attract
   (B) prohibit or forbid
   (C) make fun of
   (D) translate

   5. _____

6. *Correspond* (line 9) means _____.
   (A) to tremble
   (B) to wander aimlessly
   (C) to live in the same time or place
   (D) to communicate by letter

   6. _____

7. If something *lumbers* (line 13), it _____.
   (A) disappears suddenly
   (B) is openly brutal
   (C) moves along slowly and with difficulty
   (D) provides protection from fire

   7. _____

8. *Approximately* (line 22) means _____.
   (A) specifically
   (B) nearly
   (C) foolishly
   (D) exactly

   8. _____

9. Which word or words could best replace *inaugurated* in line 26?
   (A) began
   (B) exaggerated
   (C) crushed
   (D) brutally attacked

   9. _____

10. *Overwhelming* (line 32) means _____.
    (A) lacking power
    (B) unimportant
    (C) too great to be overcome
    (D) pleasant

    10. _____

Name _____

Lesson 4 Part B

Applying Meaning

Follow the directions below to write a sentence using a vocabulary word.

1. Describe a large crowd. Use the word *approximately*.

   _____
   _____
   _____

2. Write a sentence about a friend who lives far away. Use any form of the word *correspond*.

   _____
   _____
   _____

3. Use the word *craving* to describe a time when you ate something unusual.

   _____
   _____
   _____

4. Write a sentence about a time you were forced to choose between two things. Use the word *enticing*.

   _____
   _____
   _____

5. Write a sentence about the football season. Use any form of the word *inaugurate* in your sentence.

   _____
   _____
   _____

6. Use any form of the word *lumber* in a sentence about a fictional character.

   _____
   _____
   _____

7. Write a sentence about camping and bears. Use any form of the word *lure*.

___

8. Use the word *overwhelming* to describe a job.

___

9. Describe a time when you overcame a fear. Use the word *prod* in your sentence.

___

10. Write a sentence about a special house. Use a form of the word *reside*.

___

Mastering Meaning

One of the most famous riders of the Pony Express was Buffalo Bill, whose real name was William F. Cody. In addition to his short career carrying mail on horseback, Cody was a frontier scout and showman. Research the life of Buffalo Bill or another Wild West legend and write a short biography. Use some of the words you studied in this lesson.

Vocabulary of Saving and Spending

Lesson 5 Part A

Name _____

Whether we like it or not, money plays an important part in our lives. How much we make, how much we spend, and whether we borrow or save has an impact on how we live. In this lesson you will study 10 words related to saving and spending money.

Unlocking Meaning

Words
- credit
- currency
- economical
- financial
- frugal
- miser
- poverty
- prosperity
- spendthrift
- thrifty

Read the sentences or short passages below. Write the letter for the correct definition of the italicized vocabulary word.

1. Julie could not pay for the ring all at once, so the store agreed to let her buy it on *credit*, provided she pay at least $75 per month.
   - (A) type of money
   - (B) plan to pay over a period of time
   - (C) slight reduction in the price of an item
   - (D) explanation of an item's value

2. We found that most shops in Mexico accepted United States *currency*, but I always had trouble figuring out how much something cost in dollars.
   - (A) unusual coins
   - (B) documents needed to travel in a foreign country
   - (C) fake money
   - (D) type of money used in a country

3. After seeing the bills, Alice knew she had to be more *economical* in running the house. Comparing prices and doing without expensive food would help.
   - (A) careful in using money
   - (B) complicated
   - (C) selfish
   - (D) demanding about food

4. Before approving the plan for a new stadium, the mayor met with several *financial* experts to be sure the city could afford such an expense.
   - (A) having to do with managing money
   - (B) related to sports
   - (C) expensive
   - (D) highly paid

5. I believe in being *frugal*, but saving string and reusing paper towels is taking it a little too far for me.
   - (A) silly behavior
   - (B) foolish purchases
   - (C) careful with spending
   - (D) ignorant in money matters

1. _____

2. _____

3. _____

4.

5.

Vocabulary of Saving and Spending 19

6. The old *miser* lived in a run-down little house, but thousands of dollars were found hidden under the floor.
   (A) someone who gives money away
   (B) someone who owes a great deal of money
   (C) someone who saves money but rarely spends it
   (D) someone who buys old houses

   6. _____

7. I was struck by the beautiful skyscrapers and fountains. However, I saw many homeless people, which meant that there was much *poverty* in the city.
   (A) wealth
   (B) state of being poor
   (C) lack of care
   (D) property

   7. _____

8. Thanks to the *prosperity* in our area, few people are out of work.
   (A) shortage
   (B) business slump
   (C) good luck
   (D) business success

   8. _____

9. Margo is such a *spendthrift*. After one trip to the mall, her entire paycheck is gone.
   (A) wise shopper
   (B) person who spends money wastefully
   (C) well-paid worker
   (D) person with expensive needs

   9. _____

10. *Thrifty* buyers save their money until they can pay cash for an item and thereby avoid the cost of borrowing money.
    (A) poor
    (B) uninformed
    (C) careful with money
    (D) wasteful with money

    10. _____

20 Vocabulary of Saving and Spending

Name _____

Applying Meaning

Lesson 5 — Part B

Decide which word in parentheses best completes the sentence. Then write the sentence, adding the missing word.

1. The cost of insurance and new tires makes owning a car a _____ burden for most young people. (financial; frugal)

   _____
   _____
   _____

2. It is more _____ to make long distance calls on the weekend. (economical; financial)

   _____
   _____
   _____

3. Insisting that a penny saved is a penny earned, Benjamin Franklin was well known for his _____ ways. (spendthrift; thrifty)

   _____
   _____
   _____

4. Because I was behind on my payments, the store would not extend my _____ to make additional purchases. (credit; currency)

   _____
   _____
   _____

5. The story is about an elderly _____ who suddenly becomes generous when he realizes he is dying. (miser; spendthrift)

   _____
   _____
   _____

Each question below contains a vocabulary word from this lesson. Answer each question "yes" or "no" in the space provided.

6. Is an electrical outlet the source of *currency*?   6. _____

7. Would *poverty* cause a person to become more *frugal*?   7. _____

Vocabulary of Saving and Spending   21

8. Are empty stores and idle workers a sign of *prosperity*? 8. _____

9. Would you want a *spendthrift* to handle your money? 9. _____

10. Is *frugal* another word for *thrifty*? 10. _____

For each question you answered "no," write a sentence explaining your reason.

_____
_____
_____
_____
_____
_____
_____
_____
_____

Bonus Words

The various denominations of our currency are a source of many expressions. A dollar-a-year man is an official who gets a token payment of one dollar for his services. A penny-wise person is careful with small sums of money or other small matters. One's two cents worth is his or her opinion.

Check the Meaning: Look up the following expressions in a dictionary and write their meanings: two bits, penny ante, dollar diplomacy

The Roots -vis- and -audi-

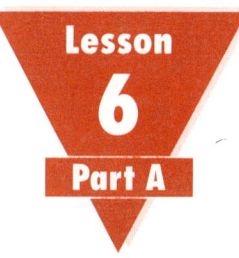

Lesson 6 Part A

Name _____

The Latin word for "to see" is *videre*. Its past participle is *visus*. This Latin word appears in numerous English words as the root -*vis*- or -*vid*-. The Latin word *audire* means "to hear" and appears as the root -*audi*- in English words. Each vocabulary word in this lesson contains one of these two roots.

Root	Meaning	English Word
-*vis*-	see	supervise
-*vid*-	see	evident
-*audi*-	hear	audible

Words
- audible
- audition
- auditorium
- auditory
- evident
- revise
- supervise
- visionary
- visor
- vista

Unlocking Meaning

A vocabulary word appears in italics in each sentence or short passage below. Find the root in the vocabulary word and think about how the word is used in the passage. Then write a definition for the vocabulary word. Compare your definition with the one in the dictionary at the back of the book.

1. The announcer's introduction of the players was barely *audible* above the noise of the cheering crowd.

   _____
   _____
   _____

2. Anyone wishing to join the school choir must complete an application and sing the school song at an *audition*.

   _____
   _____
   _____

3. All students were asked to assemble in the *auditorium* for a speech by the new superintendent.

   _____
   _____
   _____

The Roots -*vis*- and -*audi*- 23

4. Some physicians feel that listening to loud music day after day can eventually damage one's *auditory* nerves.

5. Ramona's disappointment in not making the team was *evident* from the sad look on her face.

6. After Mr. Mahdi explained how my essay could be improved, he asked me to *revise* it and turn it in next week.

7. It is my brother's job to *supervise* the cook and four waitpersons to be sure their work is done properly.

8. The committee's *visionary* plan for the new airport included runways for space shuttles.

9. The pitcher pulled down the *visor* on his cap, clenched his teeth, and glared at the batter.

10. As the hot air balloon rose above the mountain, the breathtaking *vista* of the Arizona desert came into view.

24   The Roots *-vis-* **and** *-audi-*

Name _____

Lesson 6 Part B

Applying Meaning

Decide which word in parentheses best completes the sentence. Then write the sentence, adding the missing word.

1. The fire alarm was tested to be sure it was _____ throughout the building. (audible; visionary)

   _____
   _____
   _____

2. The new information from the satellite made the weather bureau _____ its forecast for tomorrow. (supervise; revise)

   _____
   _____
   _____

3. The snow and freezing rain made it _____ that winter had finally arrived. (auditory; evident)

   _____
   _____
   _____

4. Ken's work was so well done that the owners asked him to _____ the other clerks. (revise; supervise)

   _____
   _____
   _____

5. In the distant _____ we could see the herd of buffalo moving slowly to their winter home. (visor; vista)

   _____
   _____
   _____

6. Emily failed to adjust the _____ on her cap, so she lost sight of the bird in the bright sun. (visor; vista)

   _____
   _____
   _____

The Roots -vis- and -audi-

Each question below contains at least one vocabulary word from this lesson. Answer each question "yes" or "no" in the space provided.

7. Would you go to a *visionary* doctor to have your eyes checked?　　7. _____
8. Could the drama coach hold *auditions* in an *auditorium*?　　8. _____
9. Do scientists do much of their work in an *auditory*?　　9. _____
10. Do crowded schools sometimes build *auditions* to create more classrooms?　　10. _____

For each question you answered "no," write a sentence explaining your reason.

_____
_____
_____
_____
_____
_____

Test-Taking Strategies

One type of test you may be asked to take is a test of standard English grammar and usage. The test often asks you to find the part of a sentence that contains an error. When taking such a test, always read the entire sentence before deciding on your answer. Test your answer by deciding how you would correct the error.

Practice: Write the letter for the underlined part of the sentence with an error. If there is no error, write E.

1. <u>Whenever</u> a hurricane <u>approaches</u>, <u>everyone</u> is asked to board up　　1. _____
   　　A　　　　　　　　　B　　　　　　C
   <u>their</u> windows and take shelter in the basement. <u>No Error</u>
   　D　　　　　　　　　　　　　　　　　　　　　　E

2. Mr. Chase does not approve of <u>me</u> spending so much time　　2. _____
   　　　　　　　　　　　　　　　A
   <u>deciding</u> on a science <u>project and</u> reviewing last <u>year's</u> exhibits.
   　B　　　　　　　　　C　　　　　　　　　　　　　D
   <u>No Error</u>
   　E

26　The Roots -vis- and -audi-

Assessment

Lessons 4–6

Name _____

How well do you remember the words you studied in Lessons 4–6? Take the following test covering the words from the last three lessons.

Part 1 Choose the Correct Meaning

Each question below includes a word in capital letters, followed by four words or phrases. Choose the word or phrase that is <u>closest</u> in meaning to the words in capital letters. Write the letter for your answer on the line provided.

Sample

S. FINISH	(A) enjoy	(B) complete	S. ____B____
	(C) destroy	(D) enlarge	

1. EVIDENT	(A) popular	(B) reasonable	1. _____
	(C) clear	(D) fancy	
2. CRAVE	(A) own	(B) want	2. _____
	(C) sell	(D) save	
3. THRIFTY	(A) used	(B) careful with money	3. _____
	(C) frequent	(D) overly generous	
4. AUDITION	(A) trial	(B) challenge	4. _____
	(C) checkup	(D) type of song	
5. VISTA	(A) narrow opening	(B) help	5. _____
	(C) weather	(D) view	
6. LURE	(A) impure	(B) convince	6. _____
	(C) judge	(D) attract	
7. AUDITORY	(A) quiet	(B) related to hearing	7. _____
	(C) admired	(D) darkened	
8. CORRESPOND	(A) imitate	(B) explain with examples	8. _____
	(C) hold up to ridicule	(D) communicate through writing	
9. PROSPERITY	(A) importance	(B) trust	9. _____
	(C) wealth	(D) honor	
10. PROD	(A) stop	(B) push	10. _____
	(C) support	(D) prevent	

Assessment 27

11. MISER   (A) saver   (B) cleaner   11. _____
                  (C) dieter   (D) builder

12. REVISE   (A) move   (B) take over   12. _____
                  (C) release   (D) change

13. RESIDE   (A) live in   (B) lie on   13. _____
                  (C) leave from   (D) take along

14. VISOR   (A) onlooker   (B) sunshade   14. _____
                  (C) lid   (D) glasses

15. SPENDTHRIFT   (A) miser   (B) wasteful person 15. _____
                  (C) benefactor   (D) hard worker

Part 2 Matching Words and Meaning

Match the definition in Column B with the word in Column A. Write the letter of the correct definition on the line provided.

Column A   **Column B**

16. inaugurate   a. room for a performance   16. _____
17. supervise   b. interesting or attractive   17. _____
18. auditorium   c. oversee   18. _____
19. currency   d. plan for paying over time   19. _____
20. enticing   e. move slowly   20. _____
21. approximate   f. begin   21. _____
22. visionary   g. money   22. _____
23. overwhelming   h. imaginative   23. _____
24. lumber   i. overpowering   24. _____
25. credit   j. more or less   25. _____

Context Clues: The Sciences

Lesson 7 Part A

Name _____

Meteors

On its **interplanetary** journey through space, a meteor may pass close enough to Earth to be drawn to its surface by gravity. As it collides with Earth's atmosphere, the meteor becomes so hot that it begins to melt away and fall to the surface. As it falls through the thickening atmosphere, a stream of glowing particles **emanates** from it. Most meteors burn to a fine dust soon after they **encounter** Earth's atmosphere. However, parts of larger meteors, called meteorites, may hit the surface. The largest known meteorite weighs about 60 tons. The **impact** of these meteorites leaves large circular **depressions** in the Earth's crust.

More than 120 such impact sites from meteorites and other **celestial** bodies are known to exist on Earth. Of these, the Barringer meteor crater in northern Arizona was the first to be identified. This 600-foot deep, bowl-shaped depression is surrounded by a 160-foot high rim.

Meteors can be seen on almost any clear night, but during certain times of the year they are visible in large numbers. These displays are called meteor showers. Meteor showers have been recorded for more than 900 years. Until the present century, they were the cause of **considerable** fear. Many ancient people felt these unexplained light shows **heralded** some approaching disaster. Modern science, however, has **devised** a probable explanation.

Most meteor showers are believed to be debris produced by comets that leave trails of particles behind them as they orbit the sun. The **onset** of a meteor shower is triggered when Earth's orbit passes near the course of this stream of debris. The small particles enter Earth's atmosphere at unusually high speeds, creating a bright, visible display. The largest recorded meteorite shower occurred over North America on November 12, 1833.

Today scientists can predict the time and location of a meteor shower. On a clear night a spectacular show of light can be viewed without the aid of a telescope.

Words

- celestial
- considerable
- depression
- devise
- emanate
- encounter
- herald
- impact
- interplanetary
- onset

Unlocking Meaning

Each word in this lesson's word list appears in dark type in the selection you just read. Think about how the vocabulary word is used in the selection; then write the letter for the best answer to each question.

1. *Interplanetary* (line 1) means _____.
   (A) beneath a planet's surface (B) tied to Earth
   (C) between planets (D) invisible

2. To *emanate* (line 5) is to _____.
   (A) expand (B) discard
   (C) change in an important way (D) send forth

3. If you *encounter* (line 6) something, you _____.
   (A) destroy it (B) meet it by chance
   (C) measure it (D) delay it

4. An *impact* (line 9) is a(n) _____.
   (A) sound (B) collision
   (C) object from space (D) heated rock

5. A *depression* (line 9) is a(n) _____.
   (A) area that has sunk below its surroundings (B) ice formation
   (C) period of bad weather (D) a small hill

6. Something that is *celestial* (line 12) is _____.
   (A) marked by high activity (B) soft and smooth
   (C) unknown (D) related to the sky or space

7. Which word could best replace *considerable* in line 20?
   (A) sizable (B) requested
   (C) kind and helpful (D) dishonest

8. To *herald* (line 21) is to _____.
   (A) collect (B) announce
   (C) climb (D) smooth over

9. To *devise* (line 22) is to _____.
   (A) divide (B) discard
   (C) form or create (D) break into small pieces

10. Another word for *onset* in line 25 is _____.
    (A) beginning (B) destruction
    (C) end (D) reason

Name _____

Lesson 7 Part B

Applying Meaning

Decide which word in parentheses best completes the sentence. Then write the sentence, adding the missing word.

1. I have a _____ amount of homework, so I may be late for the meeting. (celestial; considerable)

   _____
   _____
   _____

2. I spent all afternoon _____ a plan to surprise my brother on his birthday. (devising; encountering)

   _____
   _____
   _____

3. The electronic instruments on this submarine can map _____ in the ocean floor. (depressions; heralds)

   _____
   _____
   _____

4. The sounds of birds and the appearance of tulips _____ the arrival of spring. (herald; impact)

   _____
   _____
   _____

5. The director announced the launch of a(n) _____ satellite to probe the atmosphere of Mars and Jupiter. (considerable; interplanetary)

   _____
   _____
   _____

6. Sneezing and sniffling are usually signs of the _____ of a cold. (depression; onset)

   _____
   _____
   _____

Context Clues: The Sciences

7. After his camping trip, my brother related the tale of an _____ with a large bear. (encounter; onset)

8. The _____ of the collision was slight, so the air bags were not released. (impact; herald)

9. I would like a telescope so that I could view stars and other _____ bodies. (celestial; considerable)

10. The sound of laughter could be heard to _____ from the kindergarten classroom. (devise; emanate)

Mastering Meaning

Look up some information on one of the known meteorites that have struck Earth. Write a report on its location, size, and the year of its impact. Include information on the elements that make up the meteorite and how scientists are able to distinguish a meteorite from rocks found on earth. Use some of the words you learned in this lesson in your report.

Vocabulary of Quantity and Amount

Lesson 8 Part A

Name _____

How much is too much? How many are needed? Is there enough? These common questions concern quantity and amount. You probably hear them asked in one way or another several times each day. To answer such questions properly, you need words that describe the quantity or amount of something. In this lesson you will study 10 such words.

Unlocking Meaning

Words
- abundance
- adequate
- ample
- bloated
- bounteous
- deficiency
- negligible
- saturate
- scarcity
- voluminous

Read the sentences or short passages below. Write the letter for the correct definition of the italicized word.

1. The heavy winter snows and the warm spring weather caused an *abundance* of water to flow down the mountain streams.
   - (A) absence
   - (B) generous amount
   - (C) unusually small amount
   - (D) shallow pool

2. Our guide seemed certain we had brought an *adequate* supply of food for the hike. Any more would be too heavy to carry.
   - (A) uncertain
   - (B) incomplete
   - (C) dangerously low
   - (D) satisfactory

3. The perfect weather and rich soil assured us of an *ample* crop of vegetables.
   - (A) more than enough
   - (B) early
   - (C) weak or thin
   - (D) insufficient

4. After the huge meal and dessert, Harvey could hardly get his belt around his *bloated* stomach.
   - (A) empty
   - (B) swollen
   - (C) reduced
   - (D) rigid

5. Thanks to a *bounteous* harvest, the farmer was able to rent out part of his land and purchase some new machinery.
   - (A) barely enough
   - (B) puny
   - (C) plentiful
   - (D) poor

6. A *deficiency* of certain vitamins in your diet can cause you to feel weak and listless.
   - (A) large supply
   - (B) surplus
   - (C) overflow
   - (D) shortage

1. _____

2. _____

3. _____

4. _____

5. _____

6. _____

Vocabulary of Quantity and Amount 33

7. The difference in the price of the two cars was *negligible*, so we bought the one we liked best.
   (A) not worth considering (B) great
   (C) surprising (D) wide

   7. _____

8. The broken drainpipe dripped water for days and *saturated* the carpet with dirty water.
   (A) emptied (B) filled completely
   (C) drained (D) expanded

   8. _____

9. A *scarcity* of food in the area caused the buffalo to move further south where vegetation could usually be found.
   (A) abundance (B) unknown amount
   (C) lack (D) growing volume

   9. _____

10. The apartment was rather small, but it did have *voluminous* closets for storing all my winter clothes.
    (A) narrow and long (B) small in number
    (C) tall (D) having great size

    10. _____

Name _____

Lesson 8 Part B

Applying Meaning

Follow the directions below to write a sentence using a vocabulary word.

1. Describe the problems faced by a town after a disaster. Use the word *scarcity*.

   _____
   _____
   _____

2. Describe the inside of a building. Use the word *voluminous*.

   _____
   _____
   _____

3. Use *saturate* in a sentence about a thunderstorm.

   _____
   _____
   _____

4. Use *bounteous* to describe a garden someone planted.

   _____
   _____
   _____

5. Use *adequate* in a sentence about the desks in your school.

   _____
   _____
   _____

Decide which word in parentheses best completes the sentence. Then write the sentence, adding the missing word.

6. We filled the tank with gas before driving to the shore, so we would be certain to have a(n) _____ supply of fuel for the trip. (ample; negligible)

   _____
   _____
   _____

Vocabulary of Quantity and Amount

7. Contributions to the holiday toy fund were very high, so there will be a(n) _____ of happy children. (abundance; deficiency)

_____
_____
_____

8. The _____ bodies of dead fish washed up on the shore of the polluted lake. (bloated; negligible)

_____
_____
_____

9. The difference in our paychecks is _____, but somehow Jerry manages to buy expensive gifts and fine new clothes. (ample; negligible)

_____
_____
_____

10. Some scientists doubt there is life on other planets since there is a(n) _____ of oxygen on their surfaces. (abundance; deficiency)

_____
_____
_____

Using the Dictionary

Most dictionaries provide guide words to help you find a particular entry. Listed at the top of each page, these guide words tell you the first and last entry words on that page. All other words on the page come alphabetically between the two guide words. For example, if the guide words are **heart** and **height**, you know that the word **heavy** would be found on that page.

Write the entry words below that would be found on a dictionary page with these guide words:

parlor-paste

| 1. parish | 2. parrot | 3. pastry | 4. past |
| 5. pardon | 6. partial | 7. passage | 8. peace |

36 **Vocabulary of Quantity and Amount**

The Prefix re-

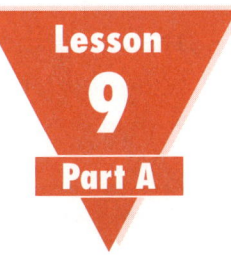

Lesson 9 Part A

Name _____

One of the most common prefixes in English is *re-*. When combined with a word or root, it adds the meaning "again" or "back" to the word or root. The *re-* prefix comes from a Latin prefix with a similar spelling and meaning. The meaning of a root may not always be known, but the prefix is always part of the meaning of the whole word.

Prefix	Meaning	English Word
re-	back	repel
re-	again	renegotiate

Unlocking Meaning

Words
- rebate
- rebuttal
- recompense
- redundant
- refrain
- reimburse
- relapse
- renegotiate
- renovate
- repel

A vocabulary word appears in italics in each sentence or short passage below. Find the prefix in the vocabulary word and think about how the word is used in the passage. Then write a definition for the vocabulary word. Compare your definition with the one in the dictionary at the back of the book.

1. The camera costs $200. However, if the receipt and a store coupon is mailed to the manufacturer, a *rebate* of $50 will be sent to the purchaser.

   _____
   _____
   _____

2. The political debate will follow strict rules. Each candidate will make a 20-minute presentation of his or her position on an issue. Then the opposing candidates will each have 10 minutes for a *rebuttal*.

   _____
   _____
   _____

3. The volunteers who collected and distributed toys at the homeless shelter found the children's smiles ample *recompense* for their work.

   _____
   _____
   _____

4. The acceptance remarks at the awards ceremony soon became *redundant*. Everyone who got an award thanked his or her parents, co-workers, and the audience.

_____
_____
_____

5. As we walked down the hall, we heard the familiar *refrain* "Three Blind Mice" coming from the kindergarten classroom again and again.

_____
_____
_____

6. Molly left her purse at home, so Liz paid for her ticket. Molly promised to *reimburse* Liz as soon as she got home.

_____
_____
_____

7. The doctor warned Meg that returning to work too soon might cause a *relapse*.

_____
_____
_____

8. The union workers pressured the owners to *renegotiate* the wages and benefits contained in their contract.

_____
_____
_____

9. The old house was in terrible condition, but rather than tear it down, the new owners decided to *renovate* it to preserve its historic charm.

_____
_____
_____

10. Hanging bars of deodorant soap throughout your garden will *repel* deer and keep them from destroying your fruit and vegetables.

_____
_____
_____

Name _____

Lesson 9 Part B

Applying Meaning

Decide which word in parentheses best completes the sentence. Then write the sentence, adding the missing word.

1. I use my own car in my sales job, so the company _____ me for my automobile expenses. (reimburses; renovates)

   _____
   _____
   _____

2. Sofia received a $1,000 _____ on her new car. (rebate; rebuttal)

   _____
   _____
   _____

3. The lawyer's stirring _____ to the evidence against her client resulted in the jury finding the defendant not guilty. (rebuttal; recompense)

   _____
   _____
   _____

4. After weeks of careful dieting, Ed suffered a serious _____ and ate a huge helping of cake and ice cream. (refrain; relapse)

   _____
   _____
   _____

5. When the returning soldiers heard the familiar _____ of "America, the Beautiful" their eyes filled with tears. (refrain; relapse)

   _____
   _____
   _____

6. Most of the spectators were _____ by the behavior of the unruly fans. (reimbursed; repelled)

   _____
   _____
   _____

The Prefix *re-*

7. The plan was to _____ the old movie palace and use it as a concert hall for the symphony. (renegotiate; renovate)

8. The small trophy hardly seemed sufficient _____ for the weeks of practice the team put in before the game. (rebuttal; recompense)

9. The teacher pointed out that the term *ATM machine* is _____ because *ATM* stands for "Automatic Teller Machine." (redundant; renovated)

10. Because he was having difficulty making the large monthly payments, Ken wanted to _____ his bank loan. (reimburse; renegotiate)

Our Living Language

Consciously or unconsciously, speakers and writers sometimes allow redundancies to creep into what they say or write. A redundancy is the habit of unnecessarily saying or writing the same thing several ways. For example, referring to something as a "free gift" is redundant. A gift is always free.

Find the redundancies in these sentences.

The bank was robbed by an armed gunman.

The meeting is planned for 10 A.M. in the morning.

Please paint the room over again.

Occurring at the same time, the simultaneous explosions rocked the city.

Every day we would see Mr. Summers taking his daily walk.

Assessment

Lessons 7-9

Name _____

How well do you remember the words you studied in Lessons 7–9? Take the following test covering the words from the last three lessons.

Part 1 Choose the Correct Meaning

Each question below includes a word in capital letters, followed by four words or phrases. Choose the word or phrase that is <u>closest</u> in meaning to the words in capital letters. Write the letter for your answer on the line provided.

Sample

S. FINISH	(A) enjoy	(B) complete	S. ____**B**____
	(C) destroy	(D) enlarge	
1. BLOATED	(A) large	(B) light	1. _____
	(C) floating	(D) swollen	
2. RENOVATE	(A) support	(B) restore	2. _____
	(C) paint	(D) reduce	
3. IMPACT	(A) forceful contact	(B) agreement	3. _____
	(C) weight	(D) damage	
4. SCARCITY	(A) lack	(B) variety	4. _____
	(C) supply	(D) nature	
5. ONSET	(A) outcome	(B) plan	5. _____
	(C) change	(D) beginning	
6. RELAPSE	(A) release	(B) improvement	6. _____
	(C) reversal	(D) delay	
7. DEVISE	(A) give	(B) save	7. _____
	(C) repeat	(D) form	
8. REPEL	(A) reject	(B) take in	8. _____
	(C) retell	(D) go beyond	
9. ABUNDANCE	(A) display	(B) choice	9. _____
	(C) plenty	(D) enough	
10. REIMBURSE	(A) pay back	(B) do over	10. _____
	(C) begin again	(D) carry along	

Assessment 41

11. CONSIDERABLE   (A) hard won   (B) thoughtful   11. _____
                   (C) large   (D) unlikely

12. REBUTTAL   (A) refund   (B) reply   12. _____
                   (C) praise   (D) view

13. INTERPLANETARY (A) level   (B) between planets   13. _____
                   (C) having to do with (D) type of geometry
                       plants

14. ENCOUNTER   (A) attack   (B) accept   14. _____
                   (C) meet   (D) forget

15. VOLUMINOUS   (A) roomy   (B) loud   15. _____
                   (C) angry   (D) important

Part 2 Matching Words and Meanings

Match the definition in Column B with the word in Column A. Write the letter of the correct definition on the line provided.

Column A	Column B	
16. redundant	a. related to the sky	16. _____
17. herald	b. repeated	17. _____
18. adequate	c. more than enough	18. _____
19. saturate	d. soak	19. _____
20. refrain	e. announce	20. _____
21. celestial	f. repeated phrase	21. _____
22. rebate	g. shortage	22. _____
23. ample	h. unimportant	23. _____
24. deficiency	i. enough	24. _____
25. negligible	j. refund	25. _____

Context Clues: The Humanities

Aesop's Fables

Although similar to other types of stories, fables are a special type of **narrative.** In **traditional** fables, such as those supposedly told by Aesop in ancient Greece, the characters are animals. The story itself is meant to teach a lesson, such as the value of some moral
5 rule or human **virtue**.

Aesop is mentioned by a number of ancient Greek authors, but it is difficult to separate fact from fiction. Most people agree that he was born a slave in the first half of the sixth century B.C. Beyond this fact, however, stories of Aesop's life are probably more **legendary**
10 than factual. As was the custom then, even those born into **servitude** were allowed to participate in public life, so even though he was a slave, Aesop may have been allowed to travel far and wide sharing his fables.

According to one somewhat questionable story, Aesop settled
15 in Sardis. There he became **acquainted** with King Croesus. Croesus thought highly of Aesop and hired him to serve as an **ambassador** of goodwill to the people. This allowed Aesop to spread the wisdom of his fables. Unfortunately, Aesop's own sense of morality led to his death.

20 Croesus sent Aesop to Delphi with gold to distribute to the citizens of that republic. When Aesop arrived, he became angry at the Delphinians' greed, so he sent the money back to Croesus. The angry Delphinians captured Aesop and immediately executed him. The people of Delphi were punished for their **rash** behavior with
25 a series of catastrophes that continued until they offered a public apology.

Whether Aesop wrote the fables credited to him or not, the stories have been retold and enjoyed for centuries. One such tale is "The Ant and the Dove." Try to figure out its moral, or lesson.

30 A very thirsty ant went down to the river for a drink. There the rushing waters carried the ant away. He was about to drown when a dove, watching from a tree branch overhanging the river, dropped a leaf into the water near the ant. The ant climbed aboard this **makeshift** raft and drifted to the
35 shore and safety. A little while later, a birdcatcher came along and began arranging twigs as a trap for the dove. The ant, realizing the birdcatcher's **scheme**, bit him in the foot. The birdcatcher's painful scream alerted the dove, who flew away.

Words
- acquainted
- ambassador
- legendary
- makeshift
- narrative
- rash
- scheme
- servitude
- traditional
- virtue

Unlocking Meaning

Each word in this lesson's word list appears in dark type in the selection you just read. Think about how the vocabulary word is used in the selection; then write the letter for the best answer to each question.

1. A *narrative* (line 2) is a(n) _____.
   (A) announcement (B) harsh wind
   (C) type of story (D) Greek musician

   1. _____

2. If something is *traditional* (line 2), it is _____.
   (A) noisy and disruptive (B) commonly agreed upon
   (C) expensive (D) odd or unusual

   2. _____

3. *Virtue* (line 5) means _____.
   (A) worthlessness (B) similarity
   (C) confusion (D) goodness

   3. _____

4. If a story is *legendary* (line 9) it is _____.
   (A) told so often it is thought to be true (B) illegal but accepted
   (C) impossible to see through (D) from a foreign source

   4. _____

5. Another word for *servitude* in line 10 is _____.
   (A) royalty (B) peace
   (C) slavery (D) wonder

   5. _____

6. *Acquainted* (line 15) means _____.
   (A) familiar (B) uncomfortable
   (C) religious (D) displeased

   6. _____

7. Which word could best replace *ambassador* in line 16?
   (A) critic (B) comedian
   (C) liar (D) representative

   7. _____

8. If you are *rash* (line 24), you are _____.
   (A) hidden from view (B) brave
   (C) hasty and reckless (D) untidy

   8. _____

9. *Makeshift* (line 34) means _____.
   (A) long lasting (B) substitute
   (C) forgettable (D) spiteful

   9. _____

10. A *scheme* (line 37) is a _____.
    (A) plan (B) place to rest
    (C) reward (D) clever statement

    10. _____

Name _____

Lesson 10 Part B

Applying Meaning

Decide which word in parentheses best completes the sentence. Then write the sentence, adding the missing word.

1. The hero of the story was a man of many _____ and great strength. (ambassadors; virtues)

   _____
   _____
   _____

2. The children loved hearing stories about the _____ heroes of the Old West. (legendary; makeshift)

   _____
   _____
   _____

3. Eleanor Roosevelt was our nation's unofficial _____ of goodwill to people at home and abroad. (ambassador; narrative)

   _____
   _____
   _____

4. The film was based on a _____ by Edgar Allen Poe that was published in 1839. (narrative; scheme)

   _____
   _____
   _____

5. He is constantly thinking up ridiculous _____ to get rich quickly, but none ever works. (narratives; schemes)

   _____
   _____
   _____

Each question below contains a vocabulary word from this lesson. Answer each question "yes" or "no" in the space provided.

6. Might a captured soldier be forced into *servitude* by his captors?   6. _____

7. Could a fallen tree be used as a *makeshift* bridge across a stream?   7. _____

Context Clues: The Humanities 45

8. Would someone who is *acquainted* with you be likely to say hello when passing you on the street?

8. _____

9. Would a cautious person continually make *rash* decisions?

9. _____

10. Is green the *traditional* color for a wedding gown?

10. _____

For each question you answered "no," write a sentence explaining your reason.

_____
_____
_____
_____
_____
_____
_____
_____
_____

Mastering Meaning

Fables often feature animal characters in stories that teach lessons, or morals. You are probably familiar with the story of the tortoise and the hare and its moral that slow and steady wins out in the end. Make up a story to teach one of the lessons below or a lesson of your own choice. Use some of the words you learned in this lesson.

Lies will eventually hurt the liar.

Money is not the most valuable thing to own.

Better to be careful than to be quick.

You don't have to be big and strong to be a hero.

Vocabulary of Geometry

Lesson 11 Part A

Name _____

Geometry is the study of the relationships between lines and surfaces. This includes the angles formed by lines and the size and shape of two- and three-dimensional figures. Geometry is used in everything from carpentry and architecture to navigation and space travel. In this lesson you will learn 10 words that are part of the special vocabulary of geometry.

Unlocking Meaning

Write a vocabulary word that fits each clue below. Then say the word and write a short definition. Compare your definition and pronunciation with those given in the dictionary at the back of the book.

1. When two roads do this there is often a stop sign or a stop light to keep cars from running into each other. It begins with the prefix *inter-*, meaning "between" or "together."

   _____
   _____
   _____

2. This is the shape of a basketball, an orange, and the world itself. It comes from the Greek word *sphaira*.

   _____
   _____
   _____

3. It begins with the prefix *circum-*, meaning "around." A fence built on this part of a yard will keep a pet inside the yard.

   _____
   _____
   _____

4. This word comes from the Greek word *parallelos*, meaning "beside one another." This word could be used to describe the lines on your writing paper.

   _____
   _____
   _____

Words

acute
circumference
congruent
cylindrical
intersect
obtuse
parallel
perpendicular
sphere
vertical

Vocabulary of Geometry 47

5. This word describes angles of less than 90°. It comes from the Latin word *acutus* but has nothing to do with being pretty.

_____
_____
_____

6. This word describes angles that measure between 90° and 180°. It comes from the Latin word *obtusus*.

_____
_____
_____

7. This word describes the relationship of two lines that form a right angle. It contains the Latin word *pendere*.

_____
_____
_____

8. The word horizontal means "level." This adjective from the Latin word *vertex* means the opposite of horizontal.

_____
_____
_____

9. Two shapes that match each other exactly are said to be this, a word that comes from *congruere*, Latin for "to agree."

_____
_____
_____

10. This adjective comes from the noun *cylinder*. It could be used to describe a pipe or a barrel.

_____
_____
_____

48 Vocabulary of Geometry

Name _____

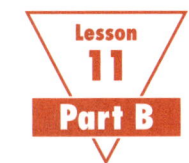

Applying Meaning

Each question below contains at least one vocabulary word from this lesson. Answer each question "yes" or "no" in the space provided.

1. Are the rails of a railroad track *parallel*? 1. _____
2. Can a square and a circle be *congruent*? 2. _____
3. Is a football a *sphere*? 3. _____
4. Is an *acute* angle smaller than an *obtuse* angle? 4. _____
5. Would it be easy to climb a *vertical* cliff? 5. _____
6. Are walls usually built around the *circumference* of a castle? 6. _____

For each question you answered "no," write a sentence explaining your reason.

_____
_____
_____
_____
_____
_____
_____
_____
_____

Decide which word in parentheses best completes the sentence. Then write the sentence, adding the missing word.

7. The tree's trunk was cut into short, _____ pieces, which were stacked next to the fireplace. (acute; cylindrical)

_____
_____
_____

8. The scientist predicted that the comet could _____ the path of the planet and cause a dangerous collision. (intersect; parallel)

_____
_____
_____

Vocabulary of Geometry

9. The afternoon winds caused the sailboat to lean slightly, so its mast was no longer _____ to the surface of the ocean. (congruent; vertical)

_____
_____
_____

10. Our instructor told us to keep our bodies _____ to the bottom of the canoe as we stepped into it. (obtuse; perpendicular)

_____
_____
_____

Cultural Literacy Note

Odysseus

According to Greek mythology, Odysseus led the Greeks in the attack on Troy. When victory finally came, Odysseus packed his ships with treasures from the defeated city and sailed for home. However, the gods decided to make it a difficult and lengthy voyage. Along the way, Odysseus and his warriors encountered lotus plants which made his men forget about home, a race of fierce, one-eyed giants called Cyclopes, a country of cannibals, and a magician who could change men into swine. In all it took 10 years for Odysseus to return to his home. Even there, he had to face enemies who wished to marry his wife and claim the throne. The name Odysseus gave modern English the word *odyssey*, meaning "a long, adventuresome voyage or trip."

Write a Story: Write a short narrative telling about an odyssey you or someone you know experienced. Title your story, "A Memorable Odyssey."

The Prefixes *ex-* and *extra-*

Name _____

The prefixes *ex-* and *extra-* can have several closely related meanings. Depending on the word or root to which they are attached, these prefixes might mean "outside," "beyond," "out of," or "away from." Each word in this lesson's word list begins with the *ex-* or *extra-* prefix.

Prefix	Meaning	Word
ex-	out of	extrude
extra-	beyond	extrasensory

Unlocking Meaning

Words
- excerpt
- exclude
- exclusive
- excursion
- extracurricular
- extradite
- extraneous
- extrasensory
- extravagant
- exultation

A vocabulary word appears in italics in each sentence or short passage below. Find the root in the vocabulary word and think about how the word is used in the passage. Then write a definition for the vocabulary word. Compare your definition with the one in the dictionary at the back of the book.

1. The magazine article included several short *excerpts* from one of President Reagan's speeches.

   _____
   _____
   _____

2. To protect the nesting birds, the new rules will *exclude* all vehicles and pets from the beaches between Memorial Day and Labor Day.

   _____
   _____
   _____

3. The movie star had promised one magazine an *exclusive* interview about her new movie. Reporters for other magazines were asked to leave.

   _____
   _____
   _____

The Prefixes *ex-* and *extra-* 51

4. Leaving the familiar world behind, Lewis and Clark began their *excursion* into the unfamiliar Louisiana Territory.

5. Students must have a C average to be allowed to participate in football, the science club, or other *extracurricular* activities.

6. The government of Mexico agreed to *extradite* the escaped prisoner. She should be returned to the United States soon.

7. Try to understand the speaker's position on the issue. Do not be misled by *extraneous* information about her brother.

8. Ed believes that animals have an *extrasensory* ability to predict earthquakes, but I think their reactions have to do with their excellent hearing.

9. My father was not usually *extravagant*, but the diamond necklace he gave Mom for their anniversary looked very expensive.

10. The *exultation* following our victory in the basketball tournament lasted well into the night.

Name _____

Lesson 12 Part B

Applying Meaning

Follow the directions below to write a sentence using a vocabulary word.

1. Describe a recent trip to a shopping mall or department store. Use the word *extravagant*.

   _____
   _____
   _____

2. Use *excerpt* in a sentence about a report you wrote or may write.

   _____
   _____
   _____

3. Write a sentence about a well-known explorer. Use the word *excursion*.

   _____
   _____
   _____

4. Use *extraneous* in a sentence about preparing for a long hike.

   _____
   _____
   _____

5. Use *extracurricular* in a sentence about a school.

   _____
   _____
   _____

Read each sentence below. Write "correct" on the answer line if the vocabulary word has been used correctly or "incorrect" if it has been used incorrectly.

6. The governor of Maine asked officials in Pennsylvania to honor his request and *extradite* the suspected murderer immediately.

   6. _____

7. There was no *exclude* for the audience's rude behavior during the movie.

   7. _____

The Prefixes *ex-* and *extra-* 53

8. June is quite *extrasensory* about losing the election, so don't mention it when you see her.

9. Before being admitted to the *exclusive* academy, a candidate must pass a test, speak a foreign language, and have the recommendation of three teachers.

10. More than 50 dealers showed off their new cars at the annual auto *exultation*.

For each word used incorrectly, write a sentence using the word properly.

_____
_____
_____
_____
_____
_____
_____
_____

Test-Taking Strategies

Tests of vocabulary sometimes ask you to choose a synonym for the word being tested. A synonym is a word with the same or nearly the same meaning. For example, *intelligent* is a synonym for *smart*. When taking this type of test, you should study each choice and eliminate any answers that are clearly wrong.

Practice: Choose the synonym for the italicized word in each sentence.

1. The skater was determined to *excel* beyond all other performers.

    (A) embarrass   (B) surpass   (C) hide   (D) imitate

2. The show of force only *exacerbated* the tensions between the hostile nations.

    (A) reduced   (B) delayed   (C) increased   (D) annoyed

3. Some felt the new law would *impinge* on the rights of others.

    (A) trespass   (B) enlarge   (C) ignore   (D) change

Assessment

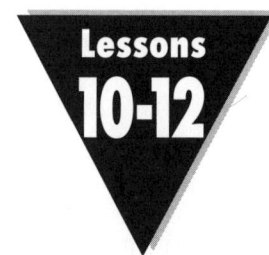

Lessons 10-12

Name _____

How well do you remember the words you studied in Lessons 10–12? Take the following test covering the words from the last three lessons.

Part 1 Choose the Correct Meaning

Each question below includes a word in capital letters, followed by four words or phrases. Choose the word or phrase that is <u>closest</u> in meaning to the word in capital letters. Write the letter for your answer on the line provided.

Sample

S. FINISH	(A) enjoy	(B) complete	S. __B__
	(C) destroy	(D) enlarge	

1. LEGENDARY	(A) level	(B) rhyming	1. _____
	(C) mythical	(D) legal	
2. EXCLUSIVE	(A) restricted	(B) richly decorated	2. _____
	(C) noisy	(D) misleading	
3. MAKESHIFT	(A) crew of workers	(B) substitute	3. _____
	(C) sideways movement	(D) perfected	
4. CONGRUENT	(A) grooved	(B) quick growing	4. _____
	(C) matching exactly	(D) easily understood	
5. EXTRANEOUS	(A) strained	(B) plain	5. _____
	(C) outside the earth	(D) unnecessary	
6. SERVITUDE	(A) morality	(B) slavery	6. _____
	(C) dinner utensils	(D) signed agreement	
7. INTERSECT	(A) secret cult	(B) interest	7. _____
	(C) cut apart	(D) cross	
8. EXCLUDE	(A) keep out	(B) shout	8. _____
	(C) stretch	(D) explode	
9. RASH	(A) reddish	(B) cautious	9. _____
	(C) reckless	(D) simple	
10. PARALLEL	(A) never crossing	(B) tied together	10. _____
	(C) unequal	(D) immovable	

Assessment **55**

11. CIRCUMFERENCE (A) important meeting (B) sound thinking   11. _____
                   (C) spiral shaped   (D) boundary

12. VIRTUE   (A) peak   (B) morality   12. _____
                   (C) hostility   (D) facial expression

13. SPHERE   (A) flat   (B) pointed   13. _____
                   (C) ball shaped   (D) hollow pipe

14. TRADITIONAL   (A) broken   (B) ancient   14. _____
                   (C) handed down   (D) oddly shaped

15. ACUTE   (A) small angle   (B) attractive   15. _____
                   (C) exact   (D) simple

Part 2 Matching Words and Meanings

Match the definition in Column B with the word in Column A. Write the letter of the correct definition on the line provided.

Column A   **Column B**

16. scheme   a. beyond the senses   16. _____
17. exultation   b. given to excess spending   17. _____
18. ambassador   c. portion   18. _____
19. cylindrical   d. rejoicing   19. _____
20. extravagant   e. deliver to another authority   20. _____
21. acquainted   f. shaped like a soup can or pipe   21. _____
22. extradite   g. story   22. _____
23. narrative   h. plot   23. _____
24. extrasensory   i. knowledgeable   24. _____
25. excerpt   j. representative   25. _____

56 Assessment

Context Clues: Social Studies

Lesson 13 Part A

Name _____

The Maya

Perhaps one of the most fascinating cultures of all time is that of the ancient Maya. Many scientists believe they had the most advanced civilization among the early peoples of the Western World. The Mayan civilization, which flourished from A.D. 250 to about A.D. 900,
5 was situated in southern Mexico and Central America. The original Maya settled and formed fishing communities along the coastline. Later they moved inland, where their **subsistence** depended on agriculture. To maintain healthy crops of corn and other grains, they developed a complex system for managing their water supply.
10 Hidden behind thick vegetation and a difficult landscape, the ruins of most ancient Mayan cities were not discovered until the 19th century. Around that time scientists began to **decipher** some of the picturelike **hieroglyphic** markings on Mayan calendars. When researchers compared the Mayan calendar with the Christian
15 calendar, they were stunned by its accuracy.
  Mayan symbols, or *glyphs*, however, did more than mark time on a calendar. Scientists determined that the differing glyphs indicated major events that occurred during the reign of various **dynasties**, the ruling families who built small empires within the Mayan nation.
20 These families passed their power on to their male children, creating an important and powerful **lineage**. From these empires came a bounty of art, architecture, and writing.
  Mayan artists produced stone sculptures, carvings, paintings, and exotic jewelry. Mayan architecture included stone and earthen homes,
25 pyramids, **shrines** devoted to Mayan gods and goddesses, and small arenas for athletic competition. Writings by Mayan scribes and priests recount the lives and deeds of nobles, astronomical details of the times, an elaborate mythology, and descriptions of religious **rituals** and other ceremonies.
30 Up until about A.D. 900, the Maya were a more or less stable civilization. Then they mysteriously abandoned the great centers of culture and began to **migrate** to other areas. Over the next several centuries the Maya fell victim to crop failures and the resulting **famines**, and to invasion, periodic wars, and European diseases.
35 The surviving cities had a **precarious** existence, yet some endured Spanish conquests and internal conflict until 1697, when the last Mayan kingdom was taken by Spain.

Words
- decipher
- dynasty
- famine
- hieroglyphic
- lineage
- migrate
- precarious
- ritual
- shrine
- subsistence

Unlocking Meaning

Each word in this lesson's word list appears in dark type in the selection you just read. Think about how the vocabulary word is used in the selection; then write the letter for the best answer to each question.

1. *Subsistence* (line 7) means _____.
    (A) athletic events   (B) conflict
    (C) ability to survive   (D) system of government

    1. _____

2. To *decipher* (line 12) is to _____.
    (A) figure out   (B) erase
    (C) hurry   (D) ridicule

    2. _____

3. A *hieroglyphic* (line 13) marking is _____.
    (A) easily understood   (B) usually unimportant
    (C) used by kings and other rulers   (D) made up of pictures or symbols

    3. _____

4. A *dynasty* (line 18) is a _____.
    (A) library of reference materials   (B) series of rulers from the same family
    (C) source of light   (D) place where a liquid is stored

    4. _____

5. Another word for *lineage* (line 21) is _____.
    (A) ancestry   (B) library
    (C) throne   (D) island

    5. _____

6. *Shrines* (line 25) are _____.
    (A) places for doing business   (B) meeting places for workers
    (C) holy or highly respected places   (D) types of fish

    6. _____

7. A *ritual* (line 28) is a _____.
    (A) false statement   (B) ceremonial act
    (C) system of lakes   (D) type of jewelry made from gold

    7. _____

8. To *migrate* (line 32) is to _____.
    (A) study carefully   (B) break into small pieces
    (C) cause great pain   (D) move from one region to another

    8. _____

9. A *famine* (line 34) is a _____.
    (A) time of great wealth   (B) type of prayer
    (C) shortage of food   (D) family event

    9. _____

10. Another word for *precarious* (line 35) is _____.
    (A) dangerous   (B) triumphant
    (C) safe   (D) happy

    10. _____

Name _____

Applying Meaning

Follow the directions below to write a sentence using a vocabulary word.

1. Write a sentence about an ancient temple. Use the word *hieroglyphic* in your sentence.

   _____
   _____
   _____

2. Describe a real or imaginary message sent during wartime. Use any form of the word *decipher*.

   _____
   _____
   _____

3. Use any form of the word *precarious* to describe the location of an object.

   _____
   _____
   _____

4. Write a sentence about a wedding. Use the word *ritual*.

   _____
   _____
   _____

5. Describe an event in history. Use any form of the word *migrate*.

   _____
   _____
   _____

Read each sentence below. Write "correct" on the answer line if the vocabulary word has been used correctly or "incorrect" if it has been used incorrectly.

6. When the lead actor became sick, another actor was called in as a *subsistence*.   6. _____

7. Queen Elizabeth I, a descendant of Henry VII, was the last of the Tudor *dynasty* that began in 1485.   7. _____

Context Clues: Social Studies   59

8. Many celebrities seeking *famine* find themselves overwhelmed by photographers and reporters.

8. _____

9. The *lineage* drawn carefully on the page formed a perfect square.

9. _____

10. Ancient civilizations often built *shrines* to honor the gods and goddesses whom they worshipped.

10. _____

For each word used incorrectly, write a sentence using the word properly.

_____
_____
_____
_____
_____
_____
_____
_____

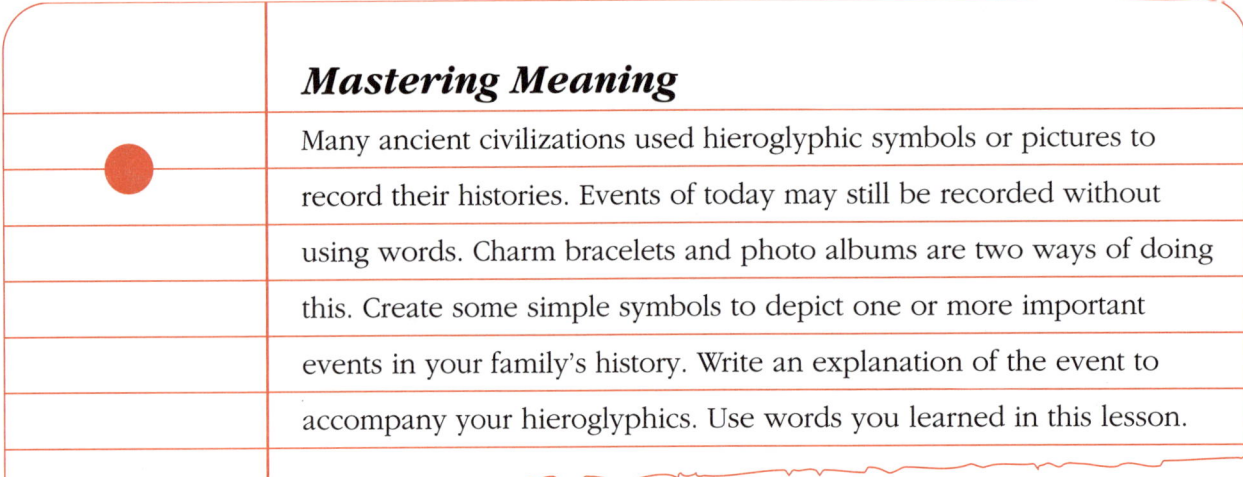

Mastering Meaning

Many ancient civilizations used hieroglyphic symbols or pictures to record their histories. Events of today may still be recorded without using words. Charm bracelets and photo albums are two ways of doing this. Create some simple symbols to depict one or more important events in your family's history. Write an explanation of the event to accompany your hieroglyphics. Use words you learned in this lesson.

Confusing Pairs

Name _____

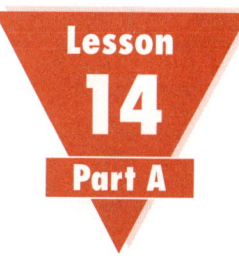

Words that sound alike or nearly alike can be confusing when reading or writing. Special attention needs to be devoted to their meaning and use. This lesson includes word pairs that are easily confused. Studying these words in pairs will help to eliminate confusion.

Unlocking Meaning

Words
- brake
- break
- coarse
- course
- council
- counsel
- formally
- formerly
- personal
- personnel

A vocabulary word appears in italics in each sentence or short passage below. Think about how the word is used in the passage. Then write a definition for the vocabulary word. Compare your definition with one in the dictionary at the back of the book.

1. Inez's car rolled down the hill because she forgot to set the emergency *brake*.

   _____
   _____
   _____

2. The X-ray showed that the hockey player suffered a small *break* in her third rib.

   _____
   _____
   _____

3. The winter weather made Herman's skin dry and *coarse*. It looked and felt like sandpaper.

   _____
   _____
   _____

4. The explorers decided to follow the *course* of the stream. They were sure it would lead them to the ocean.

   _____
   _____
   _____

Confusing Pairs 61

5. The principal formed a *council* of students and teachers to make suggestions for improvements at the school.

6. The writer sought the *counsel* of a lawyer before agreeing to sell his manuscript.

7. Even though fighting had begun the day before, Congress did not *formally* declare war on Japan until December 8, 1941.

8. Work that *formerly* took days and weeks to complete can be done in seconds on a computer.

9. Even though most critics insist that *Huckleberry Finn* is Twain's finest novel, *Tom Sawyer* is my *personal* favorite.

10. Many of the customers are military *personnel* stationed at the nearby air force base.

Name _____

Lesson 14 Part B

Applying Meaning

Decide which word in parentheses best completes the sentence. Then write the sentence, adding the missing word.

1. The choice of sausage or pepperoni pizza is a matter of one's _____ taste. (personal; personnel)

2. The president waited until the convention to _____ announce his candidacy. (formally; formerly)

3. If you take my _____, you will study regularly all semester and not try to cram for the final exam. (council; counsel)

4. Truck drivers are advised to test their _____ before starting down the steep hill. (brakes; breaks)

5. World War II changed the borders of several European countries and influenced the _____ of history. (coarse; course)

6. Until the young king reaches the age of 18, the country will be ruled by a _____ of elder statesmen. (council; counsel)

Confusing Pairs 63

7. The power outage was the result of a _____ in the main electrical line during the ice storm. (brake; break)

_____
_____
_____

8. Much of the farmwork done by tractors was _____ done by horses and oxen. (formally; formerly)

_____
_____
_____

9. Medical _____ waited for the helicopter. (personal; personnel)

_____
_____
_____

10. The _____ cloth of the potato sack made an excellent rag for scrubbing the oil off the floor. (coarse; course)

_____
_____
_____

Our Living Language

1 2 3

desert desert desert and dessert

Words that are spelled alike but have different histories and meanings are called *homographs*. For example, there are three entries in the dictionary for *desert*. If this were not confusing enough, there is another word *dessert* that has a similar meaning to one meaning of *desert*.

Write a Definition. Write a definition for each italicized word. Then use the word in a sentence.

We should never have tried to cross the hot, dry *desert*.

The criminal got his just *deserts* when he was sentenced to prison.

A true friend will not *desert* you in a time of need.

The strawberry *dessert* was the perfect end to the meal.

The Prefix un-

Lesson 15 Part A

Name _____

One of the most useful prefixes in the English language is the prefix *un-*, meaning "opposite" or "not." Sometimes the word to which it is attached can stand alone, as with *predictable* and *unpredictable*. In others, the base word has all but disappeared from English. For example, the word *couth*, which meant "known," in Old English, is rarely used today. We do, however, see and hear the word *uncouth*.

Prefix	Word	English Word
un-	accustomed	unaccustomed
un-	ruly	unruly

Unlocking Meaning

Words
unaccustomed
unbiased
uncouth
unfathomable
unflappable
ungainly
unpredictable
unruly
unsavory
unseasonable

A vocabulary word appears in italics in each sentence or short passage below. Find the prefix and base word in the vocabulary word and think about how the word is used in the passage. Then write a definition for the vocabulary word. Compare your definition with the one in the dictionary at the back of the book.

1. My Florida friends were miserable during our ski trip. Being *unaccustomed* to cold weather, they spent their time sitting by the fireplace.

   _____
   _____
   _____

2. Since everyone in Bluefield knew and liked the victim, the judge felt it would be impossible to get an *unbiased* jury there.

   _____
   _____
   _____

3. Eating with the fingers, tucking the napkin under the chin, and other *uncouth* table manners are not allowed at the military school.

   _____
   _____
   _____

4. I did well in math and algebra, but calculus was completely *unfathomable*. I needed extra help just to pass the course.

5. The rock star's appearance brought squeals of excitement from everyone but Cindy. She stayed calm and *unflappable*.

6. Don't be fooled by the *ungainly* appearance of our long-legged basketball player. She is the highest scorer on the team.

7. It is difficult to plan a trip to New England. The weather is so *unpredictable* you never know what kind of clothes to pack.

8. It took weeks to train our *unruly* puppy. He loved chewing on the furniture and barked all night.

9. The sheriff had the *unsavory* task of removing the family from their apartment after the rent went unpaid for months.

10. The *unseasonable* weather caught the orange growers by surprise, but most were able to pick their crop before the ice storm destroyed it.

Name _____

Lesson **15** Part B

Applying Meaning

Decide which word in parentheses best completes the sentence. Then write the sentence, adding the missing word.

1. Reports warned that several _____ characters were recently seen hanging around the school. (unsavory; unseasonable)

   _____
   _____
   _____

2. To get an _____ referee for the championship game, officials chose a man from the other side of the state. (unbiased; unflappable)

   _____
   _____
   _____

3. For some _____ reason, Harriet decided to turn down the scholarship and attend a small college near home. (unflappable; unfathomable)

   _____
   _____
   _____

4. It is hard to believe that the _____ young colt grew up to be a successful race horse. (unflappable; ungainly)

   _____
   _____
   _____

5. An experienced coach knows that the outcome of any baseball game is _____ right up to the final out. (ungainly; unpredictable)

   _____
   _____
   _____

Each question below contains a vocabulary word from this lesson. Answer each question "yes" or "no" in the space provided.

6. Would a king or queen be *unaccustomed* to expensive clothes, jewels, and other luxuries?

6. _____

The Prefix *un-*

7. Could an *unruly* child in the audience ruin the performance of a play or an orchestra? 7. _____

8. Would you want an *unflappable* pilot flying your plane through a storm? 8. _____

9. Would a July snowstorm be *unseasonable*? 9. _____

10. Is *uncouth* behavior expected of people at important social functions? 10. _____

For each question you answered "no," write a sentence explaining your reason.

_____

_____

_____

_____

_____

_____

_____

_____

Bonus Words

The prefix *un-* is not the only prefix that means "not." The prefix *in-* sometimes has the same meaning. It is not always easy to tell which one to use. Most short, simple words use the *un-* prefix, so we have *unfair, unwrap,* and *unusual*. However, we usually use *in-* with more complicated words like *indigestible, inappropriate,* and *incompetent*. This guideline is far from helpful, for we say *unable*, but *inability*; *unjust*, but *injustice*; and *unstable*, but *instability*.

Add the Prefix: Add *un-* or *in-* to these words. Then check a dictionary to see if you chose the correct prefix.

attached   consistent   certain   direct   expensive   common

Assessment

Lessons 13-15

Name _____

How well do you remember the words you studied in Lessons 13–15? Take the following test covering the words from the last three lessons.

Part 1 Antonyms

Each question below includes a word in capital letters, followed by four words or phrases. Choose the word or phrase that is most nearly <u>opposite</u> in meaning to the word in capital letters. Consider all choices before deciding on your answer. Write the letter for your answer on the line provided.

Sample

S. GOOD	(A) simple	(B) bad	S. __**B**__
	(C) able	(D) fast	
1. UNRULY	(A) legal	(B) orderly	1. _____
	(C) determined	(D) criminal	
2. PRECARIOUS	(A) worthless	(B) limited	2. _____
	(C) dangerous	(D) steady	
3. PERSONAL	(A) public	(B) supervisory	3. _____
	(C) hostile	(D) private	
4. COARSE	(A) smooth	(B) uneven	4. _____
	(C) path	(D) filthy	
5. UNSAVORY	(A) tasteless	(B) pleasant	5. _____
	(C) expanded	(D) educated	
6. MIGRATE	(A) relieve	(B) move	6. _____
	(C) stay	(D) improve	
7. DECIPHER	(A) fill	(B) delay	7. _____
	(C) climb	(D) confuse	
8. UNFLAPPABLE	(A) frightened	(B) loosened	8. _____
	(C) explainable	(D) ruined	
9. UNCOUTH	(A) informed	(B) well mannered	9. _____
	(C) limited	(D) sensible	
10. UNPREDICTABLE	(A) changeable	(B) desirable	10. _____
	(C) expected	(D) loud	

Assessment 69

11. FAMINE (A) masculine (B) abundance 11. _____
 (C) strength (D) hunger

12. UNGAINLY (A) sloppy (B) rising 12. _____
 (C) possibly (D) graceful

13. UNBIASED (A) unfair (B) thoughtful 13. _____
 (C) fashionable (D) heavy

14. UNFATHOMABLE (A) brave (B) mastered 14. _____
 (C) puzzling (D) shallow

15. UNACCUSTOMED (A) passable (B) quiet 15. _____
 (C) familiar (D) odd

Part 2 Matching Words and Meaning

Match the definition in Column B with the word in Column A. Write the letter of the correct definition on the line provided.

Column A	Column B	
16. formally	a. device for stopping	16. _____
17. council	b. survival	17. _____
18. dynasty	c. route	18. _____
19. subsistence	d. in the past	19. _____
20. break	e. group of advisors	20. _____
21. formerly	f. crack	21. _____
22. counsel	g. done in a proper or ceremonial way	22. _____
23. brake	h. untimely	23. _____
24. unseasonable	i. family of rulers	24. _____
25. course	j. guidance	25. _____

Context Clues: The Sciences

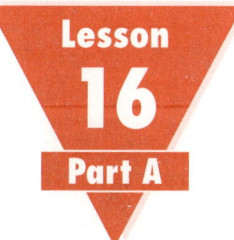

Name _____

The Rescue of the Peregrine Falcon

Few sights are as **gratifying** to American environmentalists as that of a peregrine falcon nesting high on a rocky cliff. From the 1940s until the early 1990s, the very existence of this beautiful bird of prey in North America was threatened.

5   Noted for their speed and skill in flight, peregrine falcons are small to medium-sized hawks. The diet of young peregrines consists mainly of butterflies and dragonflies. Adults **gorge** themselves on rodents or small birds that they often capture in flight with a spectacular show of skill, strength, and speed. Peregrines average about
10 50 miles per hour in normal, level flight. However, scientists believe that when peregrines swoop toward their prey, they can **attain** speeds of 200 to 300 miles per hour.

Peregrines tend to reside in treeless tundra regions such as the Arctic areas of Alaska and Canada. They construct hidden nests in
15 areas that are the natural **habitats** of birds, mice, lemmings, and other small rodents. In the late 1940s North American peregrines began to disappear at a rapid and **unaccountable** pace. By the early 1970s the decline was widespread. Eventually, scientists determined what had happened.

20 Up until 1972 Americans refused to **heed** warnings about the effect on the food chain and used DDT and other **pesticides** to control insect populations. When fish, birds, and small rodents eat insects or grain treated with pesticides, they take in the **toxins** from the pesticides. Creatures that feed on these animals eat the poisons that have
25 **accumulated** in the animals' bodies. Since peregrines eat so many birds and rodents, they were exposed to massive amounts of poison. The poisons affected the eggs that the falcons laid. The egg shells were so weak that they broke easily. Most eggs that did survive never hatched. The falcons that did hatch were too few in number to con-
30 tinue the population.

In the early 1970s environmentalists took action. The American and Arctic peregrine was placed on a list of endangered species. In 1972 laws were passed **banning** most uses of DDT. The United States Fish and Wildlife Service, along with other environmental
35 agencies, established a recovery program that reintroduced peregrines into the wild. Today thousands of peregrine pairs nest throughout Arctic North America and Alaska.

Words
accumulate
attain
ban
gorge
gratify
habitat
heed
pesticide
toxin
unaccountable

Unlocking Meaning

Each word in this lesson's word list appears in dark type in the selection you just read. Think about how the vocabulary word is used in the selection; then write the letter for the best answer to each question.

1. Something that is *gratifying* (line 1) is _____.
   - (A) manufactured
   - (B) lacking something
   - (C) satisfying
   - (D) incorrect

   1. _____

2. To *gorge* (line 7) is to _____.
   - (A) stuff with food
   - (B) lean up against
   - (C) make a guess
   - (D) push with great force

   2. _____

3. Which word or words could best replace *attain* in line 11?
   - (A) object to
   - (B) achieve
   - (C) protest
   - (D) squeeze tightly

   3. _____

4. A *habitat* (line 15) is a _____.
   - (A) vehicle
   - (B) rival or enemy
   - (C) family custom
   - (D) dwelling place

   4. _____

5. If something is *unaccountable* (line 17), it is _____.
   - (A) unexplainable
   - (B) reasonable
   - (C) filthy
   - (D) tiny

   5. _____

6. To *heed* (line 20) is to _____.
   - (A) be an example of
   - (B) seek revenge for
   - (C) pay attention to
   - (D) wish for

   6. _____

7. A *pesticide* (line 21) is a(n) _____.
   - (A) chemical used to kill pests
   - (B) opportunity for escape
   - (C) piece of secret information
   - (D) broken piece of equipment

   7. _____

8. A *toxin* (line 23) is a(n) _____.
   - (A) flowering plant
   - (B) plastic covering
   - (C) animal caught for food
   - (D) poisonous substance

   8. _____

9. *Accumulate* (line 25) means to _____.
   - (A) be extremely cold
   - (B) build up over time
   - (C) remain motionless
   - (D) be out of reach

   9. _____

10. To *ban* (line 33) is to _____.
    - (A) search for
    - (B) ask about
    - (C) discuss
    - (D) forbid

    10. _____

Context Clues: The Sciences

Name _____

Lesson 16 Part B

Applying Meaning

Decide which word in parentheses best completes the sentence. Then write the sentence, adding the missing word.

1. The sky was clear so I did not _____ the forecast of rain that I heard on the radio. (ban; heed)

2. My work at the shelter is personally _____, so payment is not necessary. (gratifying; unaccountable)

3. The musician _____ worldwide fame after years of practice and hard work. (attained; gorged)

4. The use of bottled water increased dramatically after _____ were found in the city's water supply. (habitats; toxins)

5. Most modern zoo exhibits display animals in their natural _____. (habitats; pesticides)

6. After going without food all day, he _____ himself at dinner. (attained; gorged)

Context Clues: The Sciences

7. More than 30 inches of snow _____ on the ground during the blizzard. (accumulated; heeded)

8. Instead of using a _____, the organic gardener released hundreds of ladybugs onto his plants. (pesticide; habitat)

9. Scientists were puzzled by the _____ death of dozens of young whales during the winter storm. (gratifying; unaccountable)

10. The state legislature recently passed a law that _____ smoking in all public places. (bans; heeds)

Mastering Meaning

Many species of wild animals are considered endangered or near extinction. Often, the endangered condition of these animals is due to some human activity. Choose an endangered species and write a letter to a newspaper urging private citizens and the government to take action to prevent the extinction of this animal. Use words from this lesson in your letter.

Vocabulary of Geography

Name _____

The earth includes many different types of land and water features. A special vocabulary is needed to talk about these features and to describe their locations. In this lesson you will study 10 words that are names of land or water features.

Write the vocabulary word that fits each clue below. Then say the word and write a short definition. Compare your definition with the one at the back of the book.

Words
- canal
- cape
- climate
- continent
- glacier
- hemisphere
- isthmus
- peninsula
- prairie
- strait

1. This word comes from the Latin word *paene*, meaning "almost" and *insula* meaning "island." Florida, which is "almost an island," is an example of this feature

   _____
   _____
   _____

2. It begins with the Greek word part *hemi-*, meaning "half." The earth has four of these—eastern and western and northern and southern.

   _____
   _____
   _____

3. This word comes from the Latin word *prata*, meaning "meadow." Like a meadow, this is also a good pasture for animals.

   _____
   _____
   _____

4. It comes from the Greek *klima*, meaning "earth's surface." The South has a warmer one than the North. The desert has a dry one.

   _____
   _____
   _____

5. It comes from the Latin *caput*, meaning "head." Perhaps this is because this land form looks like a head sticking out into the water.

   _____
   _____
   _____

Vocabulary of Geography

6. Africa, Asia, and Australia are examples. This word comes from the Latin *continere*, meaning "to hold together."

_____
_____
_____

7. The Latin word for ice is *glacies*. When snow piles up faster than it melts for hundreds of years, one of these is formed.

_____
_____
_____

8. From the Greek *isthmos*, the one in Panama comes between the Atlantic and Pacific Oceans. The one in Suez separates the Mediterranean Sea and the Red Sea.

_____
_____
_____

9. The Middle English word *streit* meant "narrow." It is a good place to ambush an attacking navy because the ships must crowd together to pass through.

_____
_____
_____

10. This is the word for a man-made waterway. The Panama and the Erie are two examples.

_____
_____
_____

Name _____

Lesson 17 Part B

Applying Meaning

Decide which word in parentheses best completes the sentence. Then write the sentence, adding the missing word.

1. Our trip will take us across the North American _____ from Maine to California. (continent; latitude)

   _____
   _____
   _____

2. The rising waters washed out the only road and stranded the tourists at the end of the _____. (hemisphere; peninsula)

   _____
   _____
   _____

3. The captain steered the ship carefully around the _____ adding several hundred miles to the voyage. (cape; fjord)

   _____
   _____
   _____

4. After the difficult trip over the mountains, the pioneers were happy to see the _____ spread before them. (glacier; prairie)

   _____
   _____
   _____

5. The gunboat was trapped at sea when the _____ leading to the ocean was blocked by an enemy patrol. (cape; strait)

   _____
   _____
   _____

Each question below contains at least one vocabulary word from this lesson. Answer each question "yes" or "no" in the space provided.

6. Do *glaciers* usually begin in the north and move south?   6. _____

7. Are most *canals* dug across an *isthmus*?   7. _____

Vocabulary of Geography   77

8. Is the earth divided into three *hemispheres*? 8. _____

9. Is a *climate* used to climb mountains? 9. _____

10. Does a *canal* usually shorten the distance a ship needs to travel to get from one place to another? 10. _____

For each question you answered "no," write a sentence explaining your reason.

_____
_____
_____
_____
_____
_____
_____
_____

Using the Dictionary

Does *stopping* have one or two *p*'s? Do you drop the *y* in *monkey* to form its plural? Is the *e* dropped when *-ing* is added to *hike*? A dictionary will give you these answers. Most dictionaries list words that change their spelling when endings are added or when verbs change tense. They are usually listed right after the entry word. For example, the entry word **flip** is followed by **flipped** and **flipping**. The word **begin** is followed by **began, begun,** and **beginning.**

a dictionary.

wrap + -ed. *scare* + -ing

scrappy + -est the plural of *vicinity*

the past tense of *scrub* the past tense of *shrink*

78 Vocabulary of Geography

The Prefixes be- and mal-

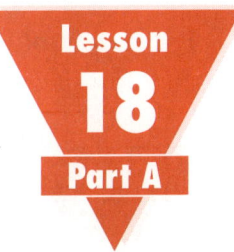

Lesson 18 Part A

Name _____

The prefix *mal-* comes from the Latin word *malus,* meaning "bad." It is usually found at the beginning of English words such as *malcontent.* The *be-* prefix has several meanings. It usually adds the meaning "completely" or "thoroughly" to a word, but sometimes the *be-* prefix adds the meaning "provide."

Prefix	Meaning	English Word
mal-	bad	malcontent
be-	completely	bemoan
be-	provide	befriend

Words

- becalm
- befriend
- befuddle
- bemoan
- maladjusted
- malcontent
- malformed
- malfunction
- malnutrition
- malpractice

Unlocking Meaning

A vocabulary word appears in italics in each sentence or short passage below. Find the root in the vocabulary word and think about how the word is used in the passage. Then write a definition for the vocabulary word. Compare your definition with the one in the dictionary at the back of the book.

1. We lost the sailboat race because the lake was suddenly *becalmed* and there was no wind at all.

   _____
   _____
   _____

2. Alone in a foreign land, the exchange student was happy when several classmates were kind enough to *befriend* him.

   _____
   _____
   _____

3. The problems with the new computers could not *befuddle* the team of experts, who fixed the breakdown in minutes.

   _____
   _____
   _____

The Prefixes be- and mal- 79

4. The coach told the team not to *bemoan* the heartbreaking loss of their last game but to look ahead to winning their next game.

5. After moving from the farm to the city, Sid felt *maladjusted* for months. City people seemed less friendly, and they even talked differently.

6. At first the British thought people in Boston were just a small group of *malcontents*. They did not realize they were starting a revolution.

7. The *malformed* fish had shriveled fins and large sores. Some scientists think this is the result of years of pollution.

8. Because of a computer's *malfunction*, the bank was unable to tell us the balance in our account or record a withdrawal.

9. When word of the wide-spread *malnutrition* in East Africa spread, the world responded with cartons of food and grain.

10. Medicine is not a perfect science, so proving that a doctor is guilty of *malpractice* is very difficult.

Name _____

Applying Meaning

Follow the directions below to write a sentence using a vocabulary word.

1. Use *malformed* in a sentence about the effects of weather.

   _____
   _____
   _____

2. Use *malfunction* in a sentence about something that might happen on an airplane.

   _____
   _____
   _____

3. Tell about a new pet. Use the word *maladjusted*.

   _____
   _____
   _____

4. Use *malcontent* in a sentence about a person in the workplace.

   _____
   _____
   _____

5. Use *becalmed* in a sentence about a day at the beach.

   _____
   _____
   _____

Read each sentence or short passage below. Write "correct" on the answer line if the vocabulary word has been used correctly or "incorrect" if it has been used incorrectly.

6. The coach was not happy with the team's performance, so he ordered extra *malpractice* after school.

   6. _____

7. The series of robberies followed no pattern and *befuddled* police for months before they solved the crimes.

   7. _____

8. Being overweight is a greater problem than *malnutrition* in most areas of the United States.

   8. _____

9. The questions on the mathematics exam completely *bemoaned* me; I doubt that I answered any correctly.

9. _____

10. Kate *befriends* every stray cat in town. They all show up at her house every morning looking for something to eat.

10. _____

For each word used incorrectly, write a sentence using the word properly.

_____
_____
_____
_____
_____
_____
_____
_____

Test-Taking Strategies

Some tests ask you to choose a word that means the opposite of a word in capital letters. These tests, called antonym tests, may try to trick you by including a synonym for the word as one of the possible answers. Remember that the test asks for the word that means the opposite of the first word.

Practice: On the line provided, write the letter for the word most nearly opposite in meaning to the word in capital letters.

1. EXPEL   (A) reject   (B) welcome   (C) explain   1. _____
                    (D) delay   (E) ignore

2. COMBINE   (A) gather   (B) condense   (C) crush   2. _____
                      (D) separate   (E) lengthen

3. SAVAGE   (A) wild   (B) calm   (C) literate   3. _____
                    (D) common   (E) civilized

The Prefixes *be-* and *mal-*

Assessment

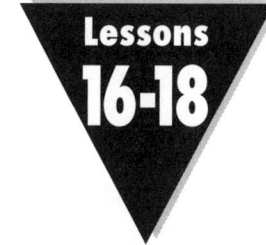

Lessons 16-18

Name _____

How well do you remember the words you studied in Lessons 16-18? Take the following test covering the words from the last three lessons.

Part 1 Choose the Correct Meaning

Each question below includes a word in capital letters, followed by four words or phrases. Choose the word or phrase that is <u>closest</u> in meaning to the word in capital letters. Write the letter for your answer on the line provided.

Sample

S. FINISH	(A) enjoy	(B) complete	S. ___**B**___
	(C) destroy	(D) enlarge	

1. PENINSULA	(A) land projecting into water	(B) narrow canyon	1. _____
	(C) imaginary line	(D) water route	

2. HABITAT	(A) religious clothes	(B) repeated action	2. _____
	(C) ceremony	(D) dwelling	

3. GLACIER	(A) shiny surface	(B) weather pattern	3. _____
	(C) large mass of ice	(D) dry area	

4. STRAIT	(A) unbending	(B) unexplored area	4. _____
	(C) lost	(D) narrow opening	

5. BAN	(A) tie together	(B) forbid	5. _____
	(C) toss	(D) ask for money	

6. UNACCOUNTABLE	(A) unexplainable	(B) carefully examined	6. _____
	(C) unpleasant	(D) highly desirable	

7. HEMISPHERE	(A) early airplane	(B) half of a globe	7. _____
	(C) heavy rain	(D) type of cloud	

8. BEFUDDLE	(A) stroke gently	(B) computer part	8. _____
	(C) confuse	(D) bend	

9. TOXIN	(A) poisonous matter	(B) talkative person	9. _____
	(C) polluted water	(D) bad-smelling substance	

10. CONTINENT	(A) government body	(B) underwater cliff	10. _____
	(C) content	(D) land mass	

11. MALFUNCTION (A) simple ceremony (B) failure 11. _____
(C) twisted shape (D) machinery

12. ISTHMUS (A) religious holiday (B) narrow strip of land 12. _____
(C) small island (D) instrument used on ships

13. MALADJUSTED (A) recently moved (B) angry 13. _____
(C) unsettled (D) poorly crafted

14. PRAIRIE (A) flat, treeless area (B) religious service 14. _____
(C) part of a river (D) place unfit for humans

15. BEMOAN (A) call out (B) refuse 15. _____
(C) waste (D) regret

Part 2 Matching Words and Meanings

Match the definition in Column B with the word in Column A. Write the letter of the correct definition on the line provided.

Column A	Column B	
16. heed	a. reach	16. _____
17. climate	b. careless or improper treatment	17. _____
18. canal	c. please	18. _____
19. attain	d. pay attention to	19. _____
20. gratify	e. typical weather	20. _____
21. malcontent	f. chemical poison	21. _____
22. gorge	g. man-made waterway	22. _____
23. accumulate	h. collect	23. _____
24. malpractice	i. stuff with food	24. _____
25. pesticide	j. one who complains often	25. _____

Context Clues: The Humanities

Lesson 19 Part A

Name _____

Pecos Bill: An American Tall Tale

Some may claim it far-fetched, but it's no **exaggeration** to say that Pecos Bill pretty much made the West what it is today. Even now, on quiet summer nights the old-timers like to **reminisce** about the day Pecos Bill **concocted** that newfangled gadget called the lasso
5 or how he taught them to round up cattle for market. Why, some claim he even made it rain once.

It all started when Bill was just a baby. When settlers moved in just 50 miles away his pa decided things were getting too crowded. He piled Bill and his 12 brothers and sisters into a wagon and set
10 out for the West. While trying to **negotiate** a rocky riverbed the wagon hit a huge rock, bouncing Bill out on the ground. Because there were so many children it was weeks before anyone missed him. All alone on the Texas plains, Bill was raised by coyotes, and he grew up strong and brave. But since he was **isolated** from peo-
15 ple, he thought he was a coyote too. Then one day a cowboy came along and **convinced** Bill that he was human.

Pecos Bill decided that he would be a cowboy. He **resolved** to be the best cowboy in the West. While other cowboys rode horses, Bill **straddled** a mountain lion. He taught men how to use spurs,
20 and he made the first ten-gallon hat. Bill and some other cowboys were out riding one day when a big rattlesnake **reared** its head in their path. The others ran off in a panic, but not Bill. He jumped from his mountain lion, grabbed the snake by the tail, and whipped it around like a rope. Then he made a loop in one end of the snake
25 and began tossing it over the necks of lizards and other animals. The cowboys were amazed at what they saw. Up until then they caught their cattle by sneaking up on them and tying their feet together before they could run off. Now they had a lasso.

Many cowboys rode wild horses, but Pecos Bill once rode a
30 cyclone. It happened the year when no rain fell. Cattle were dying of thirst. Crops had withered to a brown powder. When a whirling black cloud came spinning toward the **parched** ground Bill leaped on it and dug his spurs into its side until water began pouring down. He rode the cyclone over three states, finally falling to the
35 ground in California. The hole he left in the ground is now called Death Valley.

Words
- concoct
- convince
- exaggeration
- isolated
- negotiate
- parched
- rear
- reminisce
- resolve
- straddle

Unlocking Meaning

Each word in this lesson's word list appears in dark type in the selection you just read. Think about how the vocabulary word is used in the selection; then write the letter for the best answer to each question.

1. An *exaggeration* (line 1) can best be described as a(n) _____.
   - (A) old story
   - (B) type of western plant
   - (C) statement that enlarges on the truth
   - (D) exact statement of the truth

   1. _____

2. If you *reminisce* (line 3), you _____.
   - (A) recall the past
   - (B) argue over a small matter
   - (C) explain a confusing problem
   - (D) watch carefully

   2. _____

3. Another word for *concocted* (line 4) is _____.
   - (A) destroyed
   - (B) invented
   - (C) stretched
   - (D) entertained

   3. _____

4. If you *negotiate* (line 10) a river bed, you _____.
   - (A) remove it
   - (B) avoid it
   - (C) study it
   - (D) go over it

   4. _____

5. Another word for *isolated* (line 14) is _____.
   - (A) separated
   - (B) discarded
   - (C) escaped
   - (D) trained

   5. _____

6. To *convince* (line 16) is to _____.
   - (A) ignore
   - (B) question
   - (C) please
   - (D) persuade

   6. _____

7. Another word for *resolved* (line 17) is _____.
   - (A) denied
   - (B) decided
   - (C) whispered
   - (D) allowed

   7. _____

8. If you *straddle* (line 19) something, you _____.
   - (A) sit atop it with a leg on either side
   - (B) hold it tightly by the throat
   - (C) remove it from danger
   - (D) move out of the way of others

   8. _____

9. To *rear* (line 21) is to _____.
   - (A) smile broadly
   - (B) prevent
   - (C) raise up
   - (D) cut off

   9. _____

10. *Parched* (line 22) ground is _____.
    - (A) soaked with rain
    - (B) slippery
    - (C) dry from heat
    - (D) rocky

    10. _____

Name _____

Lesson 19 Part B

Applying Meaning

Follow the directions below to write a sentence using a vocabulary word.

1. Describe the behavior of an animal in a zoo or a rodeo. Use any form of the verb *rear*.

   _____
   _____
   _____

2. Describe a conversation with an older adult. Use any form of the word *reminisce*.

   _____
   _____
   _____

3. Use any form of the word *concoct* in a sentence about an excuse someone gave for being late to school.

   _____
   _____
   _____

4. Use *isolated* in a sentence about a camping trip.

   _____
   _____
   _____

5. Describe how your mouth sometimes feels in summer. Use the word *parched*.

   _____
   _____
   _____

6. Use *exaggeration* in a sentence about a story a child might tell.

   _____
   _____
   _____

Context Clues: The Humanities

Decide which word in parentheses best completes the sentence. Then write the sentence, adding the missing word.

7. The car slid off the road when it failed to _____ a sharp turn. (negotiate; resolve)

   _____
   _____
   _____

8. The guide suggested that we _____ the side of the inflated boat tightly as we paddled down the stream. (convince; straddle)

   _____
   _____
   _____

9. After waiting 20 minutes for someone to take his order, Fred stomped out of the restaurant and _____ never to return. (reminisced; resolved)

   _____
   _____
   _____

10. After looking for days without any luck, Dave was _____ he would never find his lost ring. (convinced; resolved)

    _____
    _____
    _____

Mastering Meaning

Many stories about Pecos Bill have been told to explain some feature of the Old West. Some attempt to explain a geographical feature, like Death Valley or the Rio Grande River. Others claim to tell how some common tool or costume came into being.

Write a Tall Tale: Write an original tall tale about Pecos Bill that explains something about the West. Use one of the ideas below or decide on a topic of your own.

How cactus came to the desert   Why the rattlesnake has rattles

How branding irons were invented

Vocabulary of Food

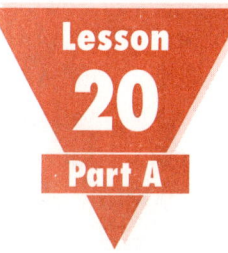

Lesson 20 Part A

Name _____

In recent years people have become more careful about what they eat. They read the labels on food packages to determine exactly what is in the food they buy. Government and private studies have heightened our awareness of the importance of food to good health and the link between certain foods and health. The 10 words in this lesson have to do with food and what it contains.

Unlocking Meaning

Read the sentences or short passages below. Write the letter for the correct definition of the italicized vocabulary word.

1. Although it is not part of the recipe, the baker puts an *additive* in the dough to make it brown more evenly.
   (A) type of baking pan
   (B) recipe for baking bread
   (C) something added to improve quality
   (D) sweet-tasting substance

2. The doctor suggested that Meg drink several glasses of milk to increase her intake of *calcium*. This will help her bones develop normally.
   (A) element found in food needed for growth
   (B) heavy material found in glass
   (C) bad tasting material found in sour milk
   (D) cause of certain diseases of the bone

3. If you expect to lose weight, you must burn up more *calories* with exercise than you consume in the food you eat.
   (A) special diet
   (B) unit for measuring energy
   (C) area reserved for preparing food
   (D) type of green vegetable

4. Too much *cholesterol* on the walls of veins or arteries is thought to lead to heart disease.
   (A) type of modern medicine
   (B) harmless bacteria
   (C) something added to food to give it better taste
   (D) fatty substance contained in some foods

5. The high *fiber* content of grain, fruits, and vegetables is good for the body. This undigested material strengthens the intestinal muscles.
   (A) the unabsorbed parts of certain foods
   (B) type of muscle
   (C) type of grain
   (D) food to be avoided

Words
- additive
- calcium
- calorie
- cholesterol
- fiber
- organic
- preservative
- protein
- starch
- vitamin

1. _____

2. _____

3. _____

4. _____

5. _____

Vocabulary of Food 89

6. More and more people have become concerned about the use of pesticides. As a result, *organic* farming has become very popular.
   (A) located in cold climates
   (B) expensive
   (C) produced without chemical fertilizers or poisons
   (D) seldom producing large or wholesome crops

   6. _____

7. The dairy refused to add a *preservative* to its milk, so it had to be sold and used quickly.
   (A) container that can be tightly sealed
   (B) impurity that enters milk when heated
   (C) an organization of dairy owners
   (D) something used to slow the spoiling process

   7. _____

8. Some nutritionists feel that growing children should get plenty of *protein,* so they recommend that children eat meat, milk, fish, or eggs every day.
   (A) substance in food that helps build and repair the body
   (B) type of food that causes aging
   (C) source of the taste in food
   (D) large serving of any food

   8. _____

9. Most meals include a serving of meat or fish, a vegetable, and a *starch*, such as potatoes, bread, or rice.
   (A) foods containing a nutrient found in nature
   (B) method of preparing food
   (C) foods imported from foreign territories
   (D) the result of overcooking

   9. _____

10. In earlier times sailors on long voyages became ill at sea because they lacked certain *vitamins* in their diets.
    (A) place where food is stored on a ship
    (B) compounds needed in small amounts to remain healthy
    (C) unsalted food
    (D) diet consisting of large amounts of fish

    10. _____

Vocabulary of Food

Name _____

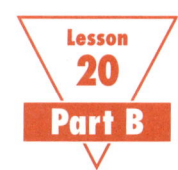

Applying Meaning

Decide which word in parentheses best completes the sentence. Then write the sentence, adding the missing word.

1. The food from _____ farms sometimes lacks the color of other foods, but the taste and nutritional value are excellent. (organic; fiber)

   _____
   _____
   _____

2. A diet of less than 2,000 _____ a day will leave many people feeling hungry. (calories; preservatives)

   _____
   _____
   _____

3. The label on the box of cereal stated that it was an all-natural food and that no _____ were used in processing. (additives; vitamins)

   _____
   _____
   _____

4. The doctor advised me to drink orange juice in order to get the _____ I need. (preservatives; vitamins)

   _____
   _____
   _____

5. The low occurrence of stomach problems in Japan may be due to the large amount of _____ in the Japanese diet. (calories; fiber)

   _____
   _____
   _____

Each question below contains at least one vocabulary word from this lesson. Answer each question "yes" or "no" in the space provided.

6. Would a *protein*-rich diet include fish and eggs?   6. _____

7. Should a person with a high *cholesterol* level eat fatty foods?   7. _____

8. Is a *starch* missing from a diet of bacon and eggs? 8. _____

9. Should *calcium* be missing in the diet of children? 9. _____

10. Are chemical *preservatives* used on *organic* farms? 10. _____

For each question you answered "no," write a sentence explaining your reason.

_____
_____
_____
_____
_____
_____
_____
_____
_____

Cultural Literacy Note

Food has always been an important part of life. It is not surprising, then, that food in one form or another is mentioned in a number of common expressions as well as in literature.

Write an Explanation: Each of the following statements mentions food. Restate each one in your own words.

He's not worth his salt.	There is no sauce like hunger.
Bring home the bacon.	He has a finger in every pie.
Enjoy your salad days.	Get to the meat of the matter.

The Suffix -logy

Lesson 21 Part A

Name _____

One of the most common English suffixes is *-logy*. It originated with the Greek word *logos*, meaning "word" or "speech." Today the *-logy* suffix is added to prefixes or roots to add the meaning "study" or "concerned with." Study the examples below.

Root or Prefix	Meaning	English Word
crimen	crime	criminology
socio-	society	sociology

Unlocking Meaning

Write the vocabulary word that fits each clue below. Then say the word and write a short definition. Compare your definition with the one in the dictionary at the back of the book.

1. This course of study takes part of its name from the Greek word *ge*, meaning "earth." Students take many field trips.

   _____
   _____
   _____

2. A religious leader must study this subject. It contains the *theo-* prefix, from the Greek word *theos*, meaning "god."

   _____
   _____
   _____

3. The Greek word *arkhaios*, meaning "ancient," can be detected in this word. Someone in this field might be found digging in ancient ruins with a tiny shovel and a brush.

   _____
   _____
   _____

4. The prefix in this word comes from the Greek *phusio*, meaning "nature." This prefix is also found in *physical* and *physician*.

   _____
   _____
   _____

Words
- archaeology
- criminology
- geology
- physiology
- psychology
- sociology
- technology
- terminology
- theology
- zoology

5. The *socio-* prefix in this word means "society." It comes from the Latin word *socius*, meaning companion.

6. The Greek *zoion*, meaning "living being," gives us the prefix in this word. The English prefix *zoo-* has a more limited meaning.

7. The ancient Greek word for skill was *tekhne*. The modern prefix refers to the special types of skills needed to use and understand computers and other scientific and industrial equipment.

8. This common prefix comes from the Greek word *psukhe*, meaning "soul" or "life." You might say it studies what isn't covered by the answer to number 4.

9. Part of the Latin word *terminus*, meaning "expression," can be seen in this word. Every occupation has these "expressions."

10. The root in this word also gives us the words *criminal* and *incriminate*.

Name _____

Applying Meaning

Decide which word in parentheses best completes the sentence. Then write the sentence, adding the missing word.

1. In my _____ class, we studied the marriage customs of several early cultures. (geology; sociology)

   _____
   _____
   _____

2. Byte, ROM, and mouse were just some of the _____ we learned when we enrolled in the computer class. (archaeology; terminology)

   _____
   _____
   _____

3. The Bible, the Book of Mormon, and the Koran were required reading for all _____ students. (technology; theology)

   _____
   _____
   _____

4. In the _____ laboratory, we examined tissue samples from frogs and snakes with a powerful microscope. (psychology; zoology)

   _____
   _____
   _____

5. Engineers must constantly study the latest _____ or they will soon find their skills are out of date. (archaeology; technology)

   _____
   _____
   _____

Each question below contains a vocabulary word from this lesson. Answer each question "yes" or "no" in the space provided.

6. Would an *archaeologist* be interested in an old piece of pottery found in the ruins of an ancient temple?   6. _____

The Suffix *-logy*   95

7. If parents are having trouble with a misbehaving child, would they discuss the problem with a child *geologist*?

7. _____

8. Might a professor of *criminology* take his class on a field trip to police headquarters to interview detectives?

8. _____

9. Could the study of *psychology* be useful to someone planning to become a marriage counselor?

9. _____

10. Are shovels and hammers necessary tools for the study of *physiology*?

10. _____

For each question you answered "no," write a sentence explaining your reason.

_____
_____
_____
_____
_____
_____
_____
_____

Bonus Words

There are more than a hundred English words with the *-logy* suffix. Some name fake sciences, like *phrenology*, the study of the shape of the head to evaluate a person's mental ability and character. Others name special interests or hobbies. *Ufology* is the study of unidentified flying objects.

Identify the Study: Look up the meanings of these studies. Write a definition for each.

| dactylology | dermatology | hematology | ophiology |
| philology | rhinology | speleology | vexillology |

Assessment

Lessons 19-21

Name _____

How well do you remember the words you studied in Lessons 19–21? Take the following test covering the words from the last three lessons.

Part 1 Choose the Correct Meaning

Each question below includes a word in capital letters, followed by four words or phrases. Choose the word or phrase that is <u>closest</u> in meaning to the word in capital letters. Write the letter for your answer on the line provided.

Sample

| S. FINISH | (A) enjoy | (B) complete | S. ___B___ |
| | (C) destroy | (D) enlarge | |

1. TERMINOLOGY	(A) study of germs	(B) words or phrases	1. _____
	(C) end of a period of time	(D) area of land	
2. ORGANIC	(A) musical	(B) healthy	2. _____
	(C) organized	(D) natural	
3. ISOLATED	(A) separate	(B) cold	3. _____
	(C) hostile	(D) reverent	
4. TECHNOLOGY	(A) advanced studies	(B) scientific knowledge used in industry	4. _____
	(C) the study of color	(D) ancient temple	
5. CALORIE	(A) element found in bones	(B) fatty tissue	5. _____
	(C) unit of energy	(D) type of thermometer	
6. CONCOCT	(A) damage	(B) delay	6. _____
	(C) conduct	(D) invent	
7. REMINISCE	(A) recall	(B) notice	7. _____
	(C) reward	(D) give up	
8. FIBER	(A) undigested parts of foods	(B) liar	8. _____
	(C) source of flavor	(D) artificial fertilizer	
9. NEGOTIATE	(A) explain	(B) defend	9. _____
	(C) go over	(D) discontinue	
10. REAR	(A) plan carefully	(B) raise up	10. _____
	(C) pull back	(D) separate	

Assessment 97

11. THEOLOGY   (A) scientific instruments   (B) the study of the earth   11. _____
                      (C) instrument for   (D) the study of god
                          measuring heat   and religion

12. EXAGGERATION   (A) overstatement   (B) decoration   12. _____
                      (C) example   (D) public show

13. PSYCHOLOGY   (A) the study of the   (B) the study of animals   13. _____
                          human body
                      (C) the study of   (D) the study of diet and
                          behavior   nutrition

14. PARCHED   (A) patched   (B) dry   14. _____
                      (C) undercooked   (D) placed side by side

15. STRADDLE   (A) choke   (B) control   15. _____
                      (C) break   (D) sit on top of

Part 2 Matching Words and Meanings

Match the definition in Column B with the word in Column A. Write the letter of the correct definition on the line provided.

Column A   **Column B**

16. additive   a. element in food necessary for good health   16. _____
17. geology   b. the study of society   17. _____
18. resolve   c. determine   18. _____
19. preservative   d. the study of early peoples and cultures   19. _____
20. convince   e. something added to improve quality   20. _____
21. sociology   f. win over   21. _____
22. cholesterol   g. the study of living creatures   22. _____
23. vitamin   h. something added to prolong freshness   23. _____
24. physiology   i. fatty substance   24. _____
25. archaeology   j. the study of earth   25. _____

Context Clues: Social Studies

Lesson 22 Part A

The Church and the State

On the surface, the First Amendment to the Constitution seems simple and **unambiguous.** It appears to **assert** quite clearly that one's religious faith is not and should not be interfered with by the government, and that the government should not support one religion over another. This principle is commonly referred to as "the separation of church and state." **Contrary** to popular belief, however, those words do not appear in the Constitution.

The earliest European settlers came to America seeking freedom to worship as they saw fit. They had little **forbearance**, however, when it came to allowing others the same freedom. For example, in Massachusetts the Puritans forced Anne Hutchinson and Roger Williams to leave the colony because their beliefs differed from those of the established faith.

In most of the early colonies religion was considered part of government. Not only was there no freedom to practice a differing faith, but the **dominant** religion of the colony **encroached** on every **facet** of one's life. A man was not allowed to vote or hold office unless he was a member of the church. The governing bodies could **impose** taxes on all members of the community for the support of the church.

Given this history, one might wonder how the United States came to require the separation of church and state. Much happened between the arrival of the Pilgrims and the drafting of the Constitution more than 150 years later. As the population increased and roads became better people were less **secluded**. This meant that people of differing views might live close together. In addition, many later settlers came to make money rather than to practice their religious beliefs. By 1787 religion was no longer considered the government's concern.

Even so, just how separate church and state are is a source of **contention**. In 1962 the Supreme Court decided that school prayer violated the First Amendment. Similar challenges have been leveled against town-sponsored Christmas displays and the phrase "under God" in the Pledge of Allegiance. Not everyone, however, agrees with these decisions. The meaning of the phrase "separation of church and state" is far from settled.

Words

- assert
- contention
- contrary
- dominant
- encroach
- facet
- forbearance
- impose
- secluded
- unambiguous

Unlocking Meaning

Each word in this lesson's word list appears in dark type in the selection you just read. Think about how the vocabulary word is used in the selection; then write the letter for the best answer to each question.

1. If a statement is *unambiguous* (line 2), it is _____.
   (A) unmistakable   (B) confusing
   (C) unnecessarily long (D) amusing

   1. _____

2. Which words best define *assert* in line 2?
   (A) deny loudly   (B) agree with
   (C) state firmly   (D) avoid cleverly

   2. _____

3. Another word for *contrary* (line 6) is _____.
   (A) agreeing   (B) opposed
   (C) exaggerating   (D) supporting

   3. _____

4. Another word for *forbearance* (line 9) is _____.
   (A) difficulty   (B) explanation
   (C) patience   (D) faith

   4. _____

5. The *dominant* (line 16) religion has _____.
   (A) few members   (B) the strictest rules
   (C) an important leader (D) the most control

   5. _____

6. To *encroach* (line 16) is to _____.
   (A) please greatly   (B) argue forcefully
   (C) avoid   (D) go beyond normal limits

   6. _____

7. Which words best define *facet* in line 16?
   (A) phase or element (B) history
   (C) illegal action   (D) business activity

   7. _____

8. To *impose* (line 18) is to _____.
   (A) suggest   (B) force
   (C) replace   (D) forbid

   8. _____

9. If something is *secluded* (line 24), it is _____.
   (A) silent   (B) afraid
   (C) alone   (D) angry

   9. _____

10. Another word for *contention* (line 30) is _____.
    (A) disagreement   (B) amusement
    (C) education   (D) laws

    10. _____

100   Context Clues: Social Studies

Name _____

Lesson 22 Part B

Applying Meaning

Decide which word in parentheses best completes the sentence. Then write the sentence, adding the missing word.

1. Little by little, the farmer enlarged his field until the neighbors accused him of _____ on their property. (asserting; encroaching)

2. The striking workers _____ their demand that they be allowed time off for family emergencies. (asserted; imposed)

3. The _____ political party in the Senate was able to vote many of its favorite bills into law. (dominant; secluded)

4. The defendant's _____ denial that he was guilty of the crime had a strong effect on the jury. (dominant; unambiguous)

5. After the speaker made her remarks, a member of the audience with a(n) _____ opinion demanded to be heard. (contrary; unambiguous)

Read each sentence or short passage below. Write "correct" on the answer line if the vocabulary word has been used correctly or "incorrect" if it has been used incorrectly.

6. After several days of rioting, the government decided to *impose* a strict curfew. No one would be permitted on the street after sunset.

6. _____

Context Clues: Social Studies 101

7. Next week our city will host a huge medical *contention*. Thousands are expected to attend.

7. _____

8. The utility company asked for the *forbearance* of its customers while it worked to restore electricity.

8. _____

9. Parts of the machinery became disabled when the small *facets* holding the gears gave way in the heat.

9. _____

10. The stolen money was hidden in a *secluded* barn not far from town.

10. _____

For each word used incorrectly, write a sentence using the word properly.

_____
_____
_____
_____
_____
_____
_____
_____

Mastering Meaning

Put yourself in the position of a Supreme Court judge. You have just heard arguments in a case about a public school teacher who was fired for refusing to remove a large pin with a religious message while teaching a class. She insists it is simply the free exercise of her religion. The school claims that since the teacher is paid with money raised by taxes, displaying this religious message violates the principle of separation of church and state. How would you decide? Make a decision and give your reasons. Use some of the words you studied in this lesson.

Vocabulary of Society

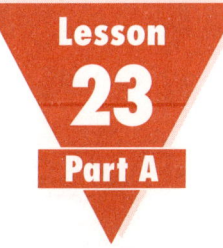

Name _____

Throughout history people have organized themselves in various ways. Sometimes they have tried to create a society where everyone is equal. At other times there have been clearly defined social classes, and moving from one social level to another was all but impossible. In this lesson you will learn 10 words that identify people and their place or role in a society.

Words
aristocrat
civilization
clan
craftsman
culture
emperor
nobility
peasant
serf
underling

Unlocking Meaning

A vocabulary word appears in italics in each sentence or short passage below. Think about how the word is used in the passage. Then write a definition for the vocabulary word. Compare your definition with the one in the dictionary at the back of the book.

1. Sir Roger Altman, a well-known *aristocrat*, inspected his land on a beautiful white horse accompanied by several servants.

   _____
   _____
   _____

2. The ancient Greek *civilization* was one of the first to produce highly developed dramas and remarkable poetry.

   _____
   _____
   _____

3. The entire O'Sullivan *clan* planned to attend a reunion this summer.

   _____
   _____
   _____

4. The shattered stained glass window will be difficult to replace. It requires a *craftsman* to create such beautiful work.

   _____
   _____
   _____

Vocabulary of Society 103

5. Jeff is an expert on Mayan *culture*. He spent years studying Mayan art, customs, and religious beliefs.

6. The *emperor* demanded that the conquered armies surrender their weapons and pledge their complete loyalty to him.

7. Having suffered at the hands of George III and the English *nobility*, the colonists refused to create such positions based on birth.

8. In the Middle Ages *peasants* had little hope of advancement. They were bound to spend their lives working land that belonged to others.

9. In 15th-century Europe, when a landowner sold his land the price often included the *serfs* and oxen that worked it.

10. When the boss asked for a report, all her *underlings* scurried about to get what she wanted before she lost her temper.

Name _____

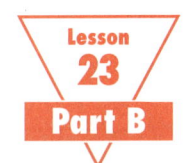

Applying Meaning

Each question below contains at least one vocabulary word from this lesson. Answer each question "yes" or "no" in the space provided.

1. Could a long-standing quarrel between two families be referred to as a feud between *clans*?

2. Is a *peasant* a member of the *nobility*?

3. Are carpenters and painters considered *craftsman* and craftswomen?

4. Is a supervisor the *underling* of his workers?

5. To study another *culture* is it necessary to examine its art and religion?

1. _____
2. _____
3. _____
4. _____
5. _____

For each question you answered "no," write a sentence explaining your reason.

_____
_____
_____
_____
_____
_____
_____
_____

Follow the directions below to write a sentence using a vocabulary word.

6. Use *civilization* in a sentence about something you studied in history.

_____
_____
_____

7. Write a sentence about slavery. Use any form of the word *serf*.

_____
_____
_____

Vocabulary of Society

8. Use any form of the word *aristocrat* in a sentence about someone you know or have read about.

_____

_____

_____

9. Use *emperor* in a sentence about someone from history.

_____

_____

_____

10. Use *nobility* in a sentence about a past or present ruler of a country.

_____

_____

_____

Bonus Words

Under can be an adverb or a preposition. It can also function as a prefix and combine with other words to change their meanings. As a result, there are many English words that include some form of *under*.

Write a Definition: Write a short definition of each of these words. Use a dictionary if necessary.

underdog   undermine   underprivileged

underrate   undercover   under-the-table

The "Big" and "Small" Affixes

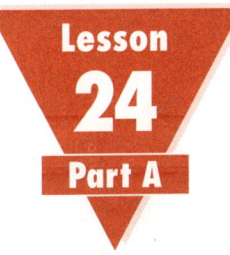

Lesson 24 Part A

Name _____

English has borrowed prefixes from Greek and Latin that add bigness or smallness to words. The prefix *mega-*, comes from the Greek word *megas*, meaning "great." The Greek word *mikros* means "small," and gives English the prefix *micro-*. The suffixes *-let, -ette,* and *-etta* come from Latin. These suffixes, called diminutives, indicate smallness or youth.

Affix	Meaning	English Word
mega-	great, large	megaphone
micro-	small	microorganism
-let	small	booklet
-ette	small	novelette

Write the vocabulary word that fits each clue below. Then write a short definition. Compare your definition with the one given in the dictionary at the back of the book.

1. Bacteria are one example. You need an instrument whose name has the same prefix to see them.

   _____
   _____
   _____

2. You might see cheerleaders using this. You should be able to hear them too.

   _____
   _____
   _____

3. The instructions for assembling and using a new appliance would be supplied in one of these, since they don't require a whole book.

   _____
   _____
   _____

4. Thousands of years ago, some people used these large stones to create monuments. We don't know of any microliths though.

   _____
   _____
   _____

Words
- booklet
- leaflet
- megabyte
- megalith
- megaphone
- microorganism
- microwave
- novelette
- operetta
- statuette

5. A novel might take days to read, but one of these will take less time.

6. Someone working for a candidate for public office might hand these out on election day. It would briefly tell people why they should vote for the candidate.

7. The Statue of Liberty is too large to be one of these.

8. This computer term means one million times more than it would if the prefix were dropped.

9. It has music and a plot. Take away the suffix, and it still has music and a plot, but it is longer and more serious.

10. It is a very small electromagnetic wave. You can cook with it.

Name _____

Lesson 24 Part B

Applying Meaning

Decide which word in parentheses best completes the sentence. Then write the sentence, adding the missing word.

1. The new software requires a minimum of two _____ of memory. (megabytes; microwaves)

   _____
   _____
   _____

2. The approaching army had a plane drop thousands of _____ urging its outnumbered enemy to surrender. (leaflets; novelettes)

   _____
   _____
   _____

3. We left the theater humming one of the lighthearted songs from the _____. (megaphone; operetta)

   _____
   _____
   _____

4. Doctors thought the illnesses were being spread by an unknown _____. (microorganism; microwave)

   _____
   _____
   _____

5. Using a _____, the film director shouted "Action!" to the actors and stage crew. (megaphone; megabyte)

   _____
   _____
   _____

6. Joseph Conrad's *The Heart of Darkness* is considered by many to be the finest _____ in English literature. (megalith; novelette)

   _____
   _____
   _____

7. The ancient ruins of Stonehenge consist of a number of _____, apparently arranged to form a type of calendar. (megabytes; megaliths)

8. The gift shop at Mount Rushmore sells _____ of the monument made of plastic or plaster. (megaliths; statuettes)

9. Every month the real estate organization publishes a _____ listing all the property for sale in the area. (booklet; novelette)

10. A _____ oven heats and cooks food in a fraction of the time a conventional oven requires. (microorganisms; microwaves)

Test-Taking Strategies

Analogy tests require you to think carefully about how two words are related to each other and then to choose the word pair that best expresses a similar relationship. Remember, you are looking for the best match.

Practice: Each question below consists of a pair of related words followed by four pairs of words or phrases. Select the pair that best expresses the same relationship as the original pair.

1. BOOK:LIBRARY:: (A) water:flavor (B) animal:zoo (C) sound:music (D) paper:pencil   1. _____

2. CANOE:RAPIDS:: (A) plane:turbulence (B) dust:road (C) propeller:motor (D) oar:boat   2. _____

3. OUTLINE:ESSAY:: (A) finger:hand (B) diagram:sentence (C) feather:bird (D) blueprint:house   3. _____

110   The "Big" and "Small" Affixes

Assessment

Lessons 22-24

Name _____

How well do you remember the words you studied in Lessons 22-24? Take the following test covering the words from the last three lessons.

Part 1 Choose the Correct Meaning

Each question below includes a word in capital letters, followed by four words or phrases. Choose the word or phrase that is <u>closest</u> in meaning to the word in capital letters. Write the letter for your answer on the line provided.

Sample

S. FINISH	(A) enjoy	(B) complete	S. __**B**__
	(C) destroy	(D) enlarge	

1. SERF	(A) deep water	(B) landlord	1. _____
	(C) ceremony	(D) slave	

| 2. MEGALITH | (A) large stone | (B) computer part | 2. _____ |
| | (C) smooth surface | (D) primitive writing | |

| 3. FACET | (A) small fastener | (B) phase | 3. _____ |
| | (C) false | (D) statement | |

| 4. CLAN | (A) secret | (B) relatives | 4. _____ |
| | (C) announcement | (D) farm worker | |

| 5. LEAFLET | (A) green plant | (B) early alphabet | 5. _____ |
| | (C) pamphlet | (D) small library | |

| 6. CONTENTION | (A) dispute | (B) large meeting | 6. _____ |
| | (C) satisfied feeling | (D) pride | |

| 7. ARISTOCRAT | (A) tourist | (B) elected official | 7. _____ |
| | (C) laborer | (D) member of a high social class | |

| 8. SECLUDED | (A) quiet | (B) set apart | 8. _____ |
| | (C) beautiful | (D) unknown | |

| 9. OPERETTA | (A) short concert | (B) type of musical entertainment | 9. _____ |
| | (C) drama set in a foreign land | (D) performance by children | |

| 10. UNDERLING | (A) bottom | (B) ocean current | 10. _____ |
| | (C) one of lower rank | (D) royal messenger | |

11. MICROORGANISM (A) tiny life form (B) small musical instrument 11. _____
    (C) scientific instrument (D) computer part

12. CIVILIZATION (A) artistic qualities 12. _____
    (B) rule by a single individual
    (C) rules that govern a community
    (D) highly developed society

13. FORBEARANCE (A) patience (B) forerunners 13. _____
    (C) skill in battle (D) system for moving large objects

14. STATUETTE (A) tall and stately (B) immovable 14. _____
    (C) small statue (D) type of memorial

15. PEASANT (A) large, colorful bird (B) farm laborer 15. _____
    (C) pleasing (D) inexpensive gift

Part 2 Matching Words and Meanings

Match the definition in Column B with the word in Column A. Write the letter of the correct definition on the line provided.

Column A   **Column B**
16. culture   a. ruling   16. _____
17. megaphone   b. invade   17. _____
18. assert   c. sound magnifier   18. _____
19. dominant   d. clearly understood   19. _____
20. unambiguous   e. opposite   20. _____
21. novelette   f. supreme ruler   21. _____
22. impose   g. habits and values of a people   22. _____
23. contrary   h. force upon   23. _____
24. encroach   i. declare   24. _____
25. emperor   j. short work of fiction   25. _____

Context Clues: The Sciences

Lesson 25 Part A

Name _____

Earthquake!

Anyone who has experienced an earthquake will never forget it. The first reaction to the sudden, violent shaking is usually confusion. Then as plates tumble from shelves and crash to the floor and lights overhead begin to sway, one begins to **comprehend** what is happening. Earthquake!

Even though scientists have learned a great deal about the cause of earthquakes, they remain one of the most unpredictable of all naturally occurring events. After **pondering** the pattern of earthquakes over long periods of time, scientists do know that earthquakes are not simply **random** events. Instead, they generally happen along what are referred to as fault lines. They also know that certain areas of the earth are more likely to produce earthquakes than others.

The outer layer of the earth, called the *crust*, is not one large, unbroken covering. It is made up of a number of huge plates. The places where these plates rub against one another are called *faults*. The movement of these surfaces against one another causes pressure to build until the plates suddenly slip free, jolting the earth. The **progressive** increase in pressure between the plates may take hundreds or even thousands of years to reach the point where the plates slip. In some cases a small **tremor** may **foretell** the arrival of a major earthquake. However, just where and when this "slipping" will occur and the **severity** of the jolt it will give the earth are impossible to pinpoint.

Their sudden occurrence and **capacity** for massive destruction have made earthquakes the cause of some of history's greatest disasters. A 1985 earthquake in Mexico City killed 1,000 people when a hospital collapsed floor upon floor. A 1971 earthquake in Peru broke huge chunks of ice from the Andes mountains. The **subsequent** mudflow caused by the melting ice killed 50,000 people. The Lisbon, Portugal, earthquake of 1755 occurred while many people were attending church services. In the **commotion** that followed the first tremor people rushed from church, only to be crushed by the collapsing walls. About 60,000 people died in that tragedy.

Words
- capacity
- commotion
- comprehend
- foretell
- ponder
- progressive
- random
- severity
- subsequent
- tremor

Unlocking Meaning

Each word in this lesson's word list appears in dark type in the selection you just read. Think about how the vocabulary word is used in the selection, then write the letter for the best answer to each question.

1. Another word for *comprehend* (line 4) is _____.
   (A) deliver (B) ignore
   (C) reject (D) understand

   1. _____

2. If you *ponder* (line 8) something you _____.
   (A) think about it thoroughly (B) expand it
   (C) desire to have it (D) divide it into parts

   2. _____

3. A *random* (line 10) event _____.
   (A) occurs in no particular pattern (B) causes great destruction
   (C) is one that is studied by scientists (D) cannot be explained

   3. _____

4. If something is *progressive* (line 18), it _____.
   (A) loses its direction (B) continues at a steady pace
   (C) has been created by heat (D) cannot be seen

   4. _____

5. Another word for *tremor* (line 20) is _____.
   (A) noise (B) explosion
   (C) shaking (D) collapse

   5. _____

6. To *foretell* (line 20) is to _____.
   (A) deny (B) excuse
   (C) predict (D) prepare for

   6. _____

7. *Severity* in line 22 means _____.
   (A) amusing (B) dark and shadowy
   (C) pleasing to the eye (D) serious or extreme

   7. _____

8. *Capacity* in line 24 means _____.
   (A) comparison (B) ability to do something
   (C) desire (D) a change in direction

   8. _____

9. Another word for *subsequent* (line 28) is _____.
   (A) slight (B) heavy
   (C) following (D) historic

   9. _____

10. A *commotion* (line 31) is a _____.
    (A) disturbance (B) discussion
    (C) prayer (D) report

    10. _____

114   Context Clues: The Sciences

Name _____

Lesson 25 Part B

Applying Meaning

Decide which word in parentheses best completes the sentence. Then write the sentence, adding the missing word.

1. At first, I had just a mild headache, but as the flu got _____ worse, I began to feel dizzy and weak. (progressively; randomly)

   _____
   _____
   _____

2. The team seemed to have an unlimited _____ for losing its games in the final seconds. (capacity; commotion)

   _____
   _____
   _____

3. Even the weather service was surprised by the _____ of the storm. (capacity; severity)

   _____
   _____
   _____

4. Once the governor vetoed the bill, all _____ efforts to get support for it failed. (random; subsequent)

   _____
   _____
   _____

5. As news of the invasion spread, the cabinet met to _____ the best response. (foretell; ponder)

   _____
   _____
   _____

Read each sentence or short passage below. Write "correct" on the answer line if the vocabulary word has been used correctly or "incorrect" if it has been used incorrectly.

6. The first singer had a deep, low voice, but the other singer was a *tremor*.

   6. _____

Context Clues: The Sciences 115

7. The magician insisted that I choose a card at *random* from the deck.

7. _____

8. Since time was limited, speakers were asked to *comprehend* their speech to no more than two minutes.

8. _____

9. No one could *foretell* the results of the close election.

9. _____

10. The teachers rushed to see what was causing the *commotion* in the hall.

10. _____

For each word used incorrectly, write a sentence using the word properly.

_____
_____
_____
_____
_____
_____
_____
_____
_____
_____

Mastering Meaning

Describe an event you experienced that caused you to become confused or fearful. It need not be anything as dramatic as an earthquake. It might be something as small as a strange noise or the unexplained disappearance of a treasured item. Describe how the event unfolded and how you felt. Use some of the words you studied in this lesson.

116 Context Clues: The Sciences

Vocabulary from Spanish

Lesson 26 Part A

Name _____

One of the strengths of the English language is its willingness to absorb words from other languages. As people arrive from other countries to make their homes here, they bring their customs, their foods, and their culture. Many of the words associated with these things have no matching English word, so the original word is kept. The words in this lesson all came from the Spanish language.

Unlocking Meaning

Words
brocade
bronco
cabana
cargo
corral
escapade
lariat
platinum
rodeo
silo

Read the sentences or short passages below. Write the letter for the correct definition of the italicized vocabulary word.

1. I could not help admiring the child's blue velvet dress. A lovely flower design could be seen on its white *brocade* collar.
   - (A) colorfully presented
   - (B) thick cloth with a raised design
   - (C) plain, inexpensive material
   - (D) pattern made from paper

2. It took 20 minutes just to get the saddle on the restless *bronco*. After seeing this, few volunteered to ride it.
   - (A) an untamed horse
   - (B) place where riding equipment is stored
   - (C) wagon pulled by two or more horses
   - (D) small desert animal

3. After relaxing on the beach for an hour, I began to feel hot. I decided to move into my *cabana* to avoid getting too much sun.
   - (A) deep water
   - (B) loose fitting clothing
   - (C) open area
   - (D) a shelter on the beach

4. The government agents thought the ship might be carrying illegal items, but an inspection of the ship's *cargo* revealed only bananas and coffee.
   - (A) the freight carried by a ship or plane
   - (B) the crew of a ship
   - (C) punishment for crimes at sea
   - (D) a government official

5. It took most of the day to find the cattle that had escaped and return them to the *corral*.
   - (A) the course followed by a river
   - (B) colorful rocks found in the ocean
   - (C) a fenced in area for holding animals
   - (D) disease affecting cattle

1. _____
2. _____
3. _____
4. _____
5. _____

Vocabulary from Spanish 117

6. Trying to circle the earth in a hot air balloon may seem like a foolish *escapade* to some, but to Ed it was a challenge.
   (A) short vacation (B) statement
   (C) judgment or opinion (D) reckless undertaking

   6. _____

7. Because of his skill with the *lariat*, the rancher was able to quickly rope the calves and hold them until they were branded.
   (A) uneven or hilly ground (B) rope with a loop for catching animals
   (C) wire used to make fences (D) tool used in farming

   7. _____

8. The jewels include several diamond and *platinum* rings and a gold crown decorated with rubies and emeralds.
   (A) unusually small (B) an expensive, silver-colored metal
   (C) common substance found in the earth (D) type of strong-tasting spice

   8. _____

9. The *rodeo* began with several roping and racing events, but everyone's favorite event, bull riding, was scheduled last.
   (A) show featuring various skills used in ranching (B) movie starring a western hero
   (C) argument over the ownership of land (D) method for shipping livestock

   9. _____

10. As the number of sheep and cows increased, the Andersons realized they would need another *silo* to hold the additional food they required.
    (A) place where animals are bought and sold (B) device used to generate electricity in rural areas
    (C) tall building used for storing food for livestock (D) type of fence found on sheep farms

    10. _____

118 Vocabulary from Spanish

Name _____

Applying Meaning

Lesson 26 Part B

Decide which word in parentheses best completes the sentence. Then write the sentence, adding the missing word.

1. All along the beach there were dozens of brightly colored _____ outlined against the blue sky and white sand. (cabanas; silos)

   _____
   _____
   _____

2. The heavy seas caused the _____ to shift, making the ship lean dangerously to one side. (brocade; cargo)

   _____
   _____
   _____

3. After Jed nearly got lost exploring the cave, his mother put an end to his _____. (escapades; rodeos)

   _____
   _____
   _____

4. Madelyn used her fine, _____ napkins only when she had special guests for dinner. (brocade; platinum)

   _____
   _____
   _____

5. When Ted saw the outline of a tall _____ in the distance, he knew he was in farm country. (cabana; silo)

   _____
   _____
   _____

Each question below contains at least one vocabulary word from this lesson. Answer each question "yes" or "no" in the space provided.

6. Would you expect paper clips to be made out of *platinum*?   6. _____

7. Might a bronco be kept in a *corral*?   7. _____

Vocabulary from Spanish 119

8. Do participants in a *rodeo* sometimes use a *lariat*? 8. _____

9. Is a *cabana* good to eat with fruit and ice cream? 9. _____

10. In case of a fire, should you try to reach the nearest *escapade*? 10. _____

For each question you answered "no," write a sentence explaining your reason.

_____
_____
_____
_____
_____
_____
_____
_____
_____

Spelling and Meaning

One way to create new words is to join together two or more existing words. The resulting word is a compound word. In some compound words, the meaning of one word is simply added to the meaning of the other. For example a *heartbeat* is the beat of a heart. Sometimes the two words create an entirely new meaning when joined together, as in *sweetheart*. A compound word may be written as one word, two words, or as a hyphenated word.

Find the Compound Words: Write five compound words by joining the words below. Check your spelling in a dictionary.

| with | red | ordinary | old | team |
| fashioned | hold | tape | mate | extra |

120 Vocabulary from Spanish

The Roots -mit- and -man-

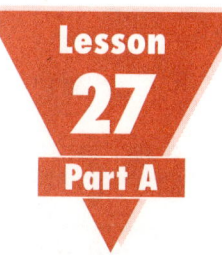

Name _____

The Latin word *mittere* means "to send." It appears as the root -mit- or -mis- in English words and is often combined with prefixes and suffixes. The Latin word *manus* means "hand." It appears as the root -man- in English words and usually keeps some element of "hand" in the meaning.

Root	Meaning	English Word
-mit-	send	commitment
-mis-	send	intermission
-man-	hand	manicure

Words

commitment
dismiss
intermission
manacle
manage
manicure
manual
manufacture
missionary
remiss

Unlocking Meaning

Write the vocabulary word that fits each clue below. Then say the word and write a short definition. Compare your definition with the one in the dictionary at the back of the book.

1. This is a name for someone who is sent on a mission, often to do religious or charity work among the poor.

   _____
   _____
   _____

2. It's not really a "cure" for sick hands, but this treatment does make the fingernails look better.

   _____
   _____
   _____

3. Teachers do this to students when the class period is over. It sends them to their next class.

   _____
   _____
   _____

4. Someone who is in charge of a store does this.

   _____
   _____

5. It begins with the prefix *inter-*, meaning "between." It refers to a time between the acts of a play when the audience is sent out.

6. Schoolwork, a job, or a marriage require a strong one of these. You might say it sends out the word that you really mean to do something.

7. This adjective has three syllables and refers to a type of work requiring the skillful use of the hands.

8. This word is formed from the Latin word for hand and the Latin word *facere*, meaning "to make."

9. This adjective begins with the *re-* prefix meaning "back." It originally meant "to send back." Now it might describe someone who fails to do homework, show up for work, or answer letters.

10. A police officer might place these on the hands of a suspected thief to keep him under control.

Name _____

Lesson 27 Part B

Applying Meaning

Decide which word in parentheses best completes the sentence. Then write the sentence, adding the missing word.

1. As the business grew, Fred had to hire an assistant to help him _____ the increasing workload. (manage; manacle)

2. The electrical failure made it impossible to work so the supervisor _____ the workers for the day. (dismissed; managed)

3. As a sign of his _____ to buying the property, the purchaser will be asked to submit a check for $500 with his offer. (commission; commitment)

4. During the war, it became necessary to _____ tires and other goods from artificial materials because importing rubber had become difficult. (manage; manufacture)

5. The hockey player's injury was treated during the _____, and amazingly, he was able to return for the final period. (commission; intermission)

The Roots -mit- and -man-

Each question below contains a vocabulary word from this lesson. Answer each question "yes" or "no" in the space provided.

6. Would you want your surgeon to possess good *manual* skills?

7. Could you purchase a *manicure* at a health center?

8. Are *manacles* usually worn during a formal dinner?

9. Would you expect a *missionary* to offer assistance to someone in another part of the world?

10. Do employers want workers who are *remiss* in performing their duties?

6. _____
7. _____
8. _____
9. _____
10. _____

For each question you answered "no," write a sentence explaining your reason.

_____
_____
_____
_____
_____

Our Living Language

macabre

During the Middle Ages a popular form of drama was the morality play. As the name suggests, these plays were intended to teach a proper moral lesson. The characters had such obvious names as Sin, Good Deeds, or Good Man. One of the most common characters was Death, frequently represented in paintings as a gruesome skeleton. In the morality plays, Death would frequently lead his human victims to their doom with an eerie dance called the *danse macabre*, a French phrase meaning "dance of death." We still use *macabre* as an adjective to suggest the horrors of death and decaying corpses.

Write a Report: Edgar Allan Poe and Stephen King are two writers who specialize in the macabre. A number of movies also fit this category. Write a short essay explaining why a particular story or movie qualifies as a macabre tale. Use some of the words you studied in this lesson.

Assessment

Lessons 25-27

Name _____

How well do you remember the words you studied in Lessons 25–27? Take the following test covering the words from the last three lessons.

Part 1 Choose the Correct Meaning

Each question below includes a word in capital letters, followed by four words or phrases. Choose the word or phrase that is <u>closest</u> in meaning to the word in capital letters. Write the letter for your answer on the line provided.

Sample

S. FINISH	(A) enjoy	(B) complete	S. ___**B**___
	(C) destroy	(D) enlarge	

1. SUBSEQUENT	(A) substitute	(B) following	1. _____
	(C) foolish	(D) underpriced	
2. CABANA	(A) shelter	(B) tropical fruit	2. _____
	(C) restaurant	(D) vault	
3. MANUAL	(A) mechanical	(B) Spanish costume	3. _____
	(C) handcuff	(D) done with the hands	
4. COMMOTION	(A) disturbance	(B) small cabinet	4. _____
	(C) closeness	(D) companion	
5. ESCAPADE	(A) path of a river	(B) theft	5. _____
	(C) daring adventure	(D) emergency exit	
6. REMISS	(A) mistaken	(B) neglectful	6. _____
	(C) relieved	(D) broken	
7. BROCADE	(A) heavy cloth	(B) farming equipment	7. _____
	(C) twisted together	(D) desert plant	
8. PONDER	(A) weigh down	(B) conquer	8. _____
	(C) explain	(D) think	
9. DISMISS	(A) connect	(B) explain	9. _____
	(C) message	(D) send away	
10. CAPACITY	(A) ability to perform a task	(B) strength	10. _____
	(C) unfair comparison	(D) the act of surrendering	

Assessment 125

11. CARGO (A) officer on a ship (B) freight 11. _____
 (C) heavy covering (D) large container

12. MANAGE (A) display (B) direct 12. _____
 (C) judge (D) split into parts

13. FORETELL (A) predict (B) mislead 13. _____
 (C) condemn (D) deliver

14. RANDOM (A) tightly wrapped (B) brightly colored 14. _____
 (C) by chance (D) speedy

15. MANICURE (A) Asian medicine (B) troop movements 15. _____
 (C) person who models clothes (D) grooming for the fingernails

Part 2 Matching Words and Meanings

Match the definition in Column B with the word in Column A. Write the letter of the correct definition on the line provided.

Column A   **Column B**

16. commitment   a. shaking   16. _____
17. tremor   b. religious representative   17. _____
18. severity   c. rope with a loop   18. _____
19. comprehend   d. promise   19. _____
20. corral   e. fenced area   20. _____
21. silo   f. understand   21. _____
22. missionary   g. handcuff   22. _____
23. manacle   h. slowly advancing   23. _____
24. progressive   i. harshness   24. _____
25. lariat   j. farm building   25. _____

Context Clues: The Humanities

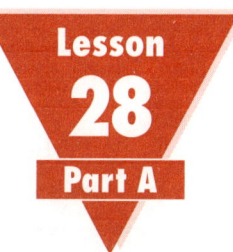

Name _____

The Arthurian Legend

What mental images do you get when you think of King Arthur and the Knights of the Round Table? For most people, the mention of King Arthur **evokes** pictures of virtuous knights in polished armor riding magnificent horses in search of adventure. However, there is no firm evidence that King Arthur ever really existed. If he did, he was probably not a king and was most certainly not named Arthur. If such a person lived at all, he was probably a Welsh warrior who fought the Germanic **aggressors** in the fifth century. If so, this was hundreds of years before the age of medieval knights.

This **nebulous** history has **provoked** an enormous number of Arthurian legends. It allowed generations of **anonymous** storytellers to enlarge on what few "facts" were known about this defender of their island. Audiences readily accepted these **yarns** of a native hero and added to them as they were passed along. Like some of our own stories about George Washington and Paul Revere, the stories gave Arthur all the qualities that the society held in high **esteem**. Consequently, King Arthur is portrayed as possessing the chivalrous qualities of the Middle Ages—bravery, courtesy, honor, and gallantry toward women. Also, since Arthur fought against heathen invaders, the stories took on a religious **aspect**. The broad **assortment** of stories about King Arthur are a mixture of history, legend, fairy tale, and moral lesson.

According to the legend, Arthur was the son of King Uther Pendragon, but he was raised by Merlin the magician and Sir Hector. Arthur proved his claim to the throne by pulling a sword, the magic Excalibur, from a great stone, something no one else could do. King Arthur and Queen Guinevere held court at Camelot. There the knights sat as equals at a round table. Conflict arose in this peaceful kingdom when Arthur's nephew, Mordred, hatched a **sinister** plot to overthrow Arthur. Mordred was slain in the ensuing battle, and Arthur was mortally wounded. His body was taken to an island where he supposedly would be healed and return to continue his reign.

Narrative poems, great operas, and even Broadway musicals have been based on the Arthurian legend. Few people really care whether a King Arthur truly existed. The stories are alive.

Words
- aggressor
- anonymous
- aspect
- assortment
- esteem
- evoke
- nebulous
- provoke
- sinister
- yarn

Unlocking Meaning

Each word in this lesson's word list appears in dark type in the selection you just read. Think about how the vocabulary word is used in the selection; then write the letter for the best answer to each question.

1. To *evoke* (line 3) is to _____.
   (A) cancel
   (B) throw away
   (C) call forth
   (D) hold back

   1. _____

2. An *aggressor* (line 8) is a(n) _____.
   (A) attacker
   (B) type of musician
   (C) weapon used by knights
   (D) hero

   2. _____

3. A *nebulous* (line 10) history is one that is _____.
   (A) clear and accurate
   (B) told by traveling entertainers
   (C) written by monks
   (D) vague

   3. _____

4. Another word for *provoked* (line 10) is _____.
   (A) denied
   (B) ridiculed
   (C) arranged
   (D) caused

   4. _____

5. An *anonymous* (line 11) storyteller is _____.
   (A) awkward
   (B) unnamed
   (C) foreign
   (D) boring

   5. _____

6. A *yarn* (line 13) is a(n) _____.
   (A) story
   (B) early type of music
   (C) warm clothing
   (D) heroic action

   6. _____

7. Another word for *esteem* (line 16) is _____.
   (A) desire
   (B) hate
   (C) regard
   (D) foolishness

   7. _____

8. *Aspect* (line 20) can best be defined as _____.
   (A) a happy ending to a story
   (B) a way of looking at something
   (C) childish behavior
   (D) a building for holding religious services

   8. _____

9. Another word for *assortment* (line 20) is _____.
   (A) humor
   (B) division
   (C) review
   (D) variety

   9. _____

10. A *sinister* (line 30) plot _____.
    (A) suggests evil
    (B) is carefully planned
    (C) cannot be stopped
    (D) is known to everyone

    10. _____

Name _____

Lesson 28 Part B

Applying Meaning

Decide which word in parentheses best completes the sentence. Then write the sentence, adding the missing word.

1. The charity received a large donation from a(n) _____ donor who wanted to avoid publicity. (anonymous; sinister)

   _____
   _____
   _____

2. The delegates to the United Nations voted to condemn the _____ and send help to those in need. (aggressor; aspect)

   _____
   _____
   _____

3. The _____ answers of the woman claiming the reward made the police officer suspicious. (anonymous; nebulous)

   _____
   _____
   _____

4. As the scene closed, the villain gave a _____ smile to the audience and said, "I'll be back." (nebulous; sinister)

   _____
   _____
   _____

5. The produce stand offered an _____ of fresh fruits and vegetables. (aspect; assortment)

   _____
   _____
   _____

Follow the directions below to write a sentence using a vocabulary word.

6. Use any form of the word *aspect* in a sentence about the coach of an athletic team.

   _____
   _____
   _____

7. Write a sentence about an elderly sea captain. Use any form of the word *yarn*.

   _____
   _____
   _____

8. Write a sentence about the effect seeing or hearing something had on you. Use any form of the word *evoke*.

   _____
   _____
   _____

9. Use *esteem* in a sentence about a historically important person.

   _____
   _____
   _____

10. Use any form of the word *provoke* in a sentence about an entertainer and his or her audience.

    _____
    _____
    _____

Mastering Meaning

Recall or create a legend about a real American that has an element of truth in it but goes beyond known facts. Some possible characters include Davy Crockett, Nellie Bly, Abraham Lincoln, Pocahontas, and Joe Louis. Use some of the words studied in this lesson in your story.

Vocabulary of the Sea

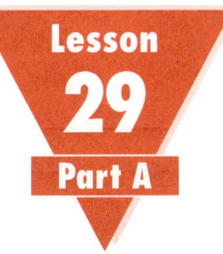

Lesson 29 Part A

Name _____

Like people who work in any occupation or setting, the men and women who sail the sea have a special vocabulary for the things they need to talk or write about. Most of us don't know the words for parts of a boat or for the surface on the bottom of a body of water. To people sailing boats or ships, however, words like these are vital for precise communication. In this lesson you will learn ten words associated with boats and the sea.

Words
- ballast
- bow
- capsize
- knot
- leeward
- scuttle
- shoals
- starboard
- stern
- windward

Unlocking Meaning

Read the sentences or short passages below. Write the letter for the correct definition of the italicized vocabulary word.

1. As the storm approached, the captain ordered additional *ballast* be taken on to steady the ship and reduce the danger of overturning.
   - (A) deck hands with little experience at sea
   - (B) heavy material carried in the lower part of a ship
   - (C) electronic equipment used to spot other ships in the area
   - (D) the cabin occupied by the captain

2. As the boat inched through the thick fog, Beth stood at the *bow* so she could warn the pilot of any rocks or boats in their path.
   - (A) part of the sail
   - (B) cargo area
   - (C) front of a boat or ship
   - (D) side of the boat facing the wind

3. A sudden gust of wind caused the sailboat to *capsize*, spilling the three aboard into the icy cold water.
   - (A) gain speed
   - (B) overturn
   - (C) turn around
   - (D) become lost

4. The captain reduced the freighter's speed to 5 *knots* as it approached the narrow canal. This allowed smaller boats time to move away from its wake.
   - (A) sound produced by a ship's horn
   - (B) measurement used to describe a ship's engine
   - (C) ropes used to raise flags
   - (D) unit of speed used by boats

5. As the wind and rain grew to hurricane strength, the residents took shelter behind a barrier on the *leeward* side of the island.
   - (A) direction toward which the wind is blowing
   - (B) without trees or other growth
   - (C) covered with water
   - (D) unprotected

1. _____

2. _____

3. _____

4. _____

5. _____

Vocabulary of the Sea 131

6. Fearing that it would fall into Union hands and be used against them, the Confederates decided to *scuttle* the Merrimac by flooding its hull.
   (A) enlarge (B) attack
   (C) strengthen (D) sink

   6. _____

7. The Coast Guard warned boaters that *shoals* near the island's east shore had caused several boats to run aground.
   (A) type of fish
   (B) large ship used to transport heavy loads
   (C) shallow area in a body of water
   (D) system for communicating at sea

   7. _____

8. As we left Boston Harbor and turned south, I could see the city skyline sparkling off the *starboard* side of the ship.
   (A) the top of a ship's mast
   (B) the right side of a ship as one faces forward
   (C) area reserved for passengers
   (D) lights used by a ship when sailing at night

   8. _____

9. Boaters participating in the parade were told not to get any closer than 50 feet from the *stern* of the boat ahead of them.
   (A) the part of a boat that lies beneath the water
   (B) the rear part of a boat
   (C) a rope used to link boats in a parade
   (D) an electronic device used in steering a boat

   9. _____

10. Thanks to the protection of the mountain, the storm had little effect, but the heavy surf on the *windward* side of the island caused considerable damage to the beaches.
    (A) direction from which the wind blows
    (B) having little value
    (C) beautiful
    (D) able to provide shelter

    10. _____

132 Vocabulary of the Sea

Name _____

Lesson 29 Part B

Applying Meaning

Decide which word in parentheses best completes the sentence. Then write the sentence, adding the missing word.

1. As the _____ of the winning sailboat crossed the finish line, the judges shot a flare into the air. (ballast; bow)

2. When a whale appeared off to our right, everyone crowded to the rail on the _____ side of the boat. (leeward; starboard)

3. The river had carried so much mud and sand to the sea that numerous _____ had formed near its mouth. (knots; shoals)

4. By increasing his speed to 12 _____, the captain calculated he would arrive in New Orleans an hour early. (knots; sterns)

5. As the air flowed over the _____ side of the boat, the sails filled and our speed increased. (leeward; windward)

6. If the winds on an island usually come from the northeast a _____ beach would be one on the southwest side. (leeward; windward)

Vocabulary of the Sea

Each question below contains at least one vocabulary word from this lesson. Answer each question "yes" or "no" in the space provided.

7. Is a ship's length the distance from its *bow* to its stern?

7. _____

8. Would an experienced captain be expected to *scuttle* his ship during a voyage?

8. _____

9. Could adding more *ballast* help a ship get through dangerous shoals?

9. _____

10. Is it possible for a huge wave to *capsize* a boat?

10. _____

For each question you answered "no," write a sentence explaining your reason.

_____
_____
_____
_____
_____
_____
_____
_____
_____
_____

Using the Dictionary

Some words have several meanings. If a word has more than one meaning, dictionaries will number each meaning. Study this example:

match (mach) n. **1.** Someone or something that is identical or nearly identical to another person or thing. **2.** Someone or something that goes well with another. *Her shoes match her purse.* **3.** Something that is equal to another. *Before the first half ended, the team knew it had met its match.* **4.** A contest, usually an athletic contest. *The tennis match drew a large crowd.*

Write a Sentence: Look up the following words in a dictionary. For each word, write a sentence using two of the meanings given.

print   strong   firm   issue

Related Words

Name _____

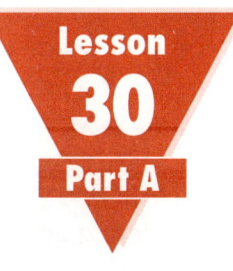

Lesson 30 Part A

Most words can be changed from a verb to a noun by adding a suffix. For some words, their pronunciation and spelling change when the noun suffix is added. Some words that seem to be different can actually be related in meaning. In this lesson you will study five such pairs of words with related meanings.

Verb	Noun
consume	consumption
deceive	deception

Unlocking Meaning

Each short passage below contains two italicized words that are related in meaning. Read each passage and think about how the words are used. Then write the letters for the correct answers to the questions.

Many Americans *consume* more fat than they should with their meals. Doctors advise us to reduce our *consumption* of fatty foods to improve our health.

1. To *consume* is to _____.
   - (A) remove
   - (B) make longer
   - (C) eat
   - (D) explain

2. *Consumption* is _____.
   - (A) the act of eating
   - (B) the act of removing
   - (C) an explanation
   - (D) the act of making longer

The army faked an attack on its southern defenses in order to *deceive* the enemy. A spy had uncovered the plan, however, and the *deception* failed.

3. Another word for *deceive* is _____.
   - (A) encourage
   - (B) delay
   - (C) observe
   - (D) trick

4. A *deception* is _____.
   - (A) a trick
   - (B) a delay
   - (C) an observation
   - (D) encouragement

Words
- consume
- consumption
- deceive
- deception
- perceive
- perception
- presume
- presumption
- redeem
- redemption

1. _____

2. _____

3. _____

4. _____

Related Words 135

Even after hours at the microscope, I could not *perceive* any difference between the two plant cells. The teacher suggested I take a break. Perhaps in an hour my *perception* would improve.

5. If you *perceive* something, you _____.
   (A) cut it apart carefully
   (B) become aware of it through observation
   (C) conceal it from public view
   (D) expose it to others

   5. _____

6. Another word for *perception* is _____.
   (A) fragment
   (B) exposure
   (C) shield
   (D) understanding

   6. _____

I *presumed* that the test would be on Friday, as always, but my *presumption* proved to be wrong. The test was given on Thursday.

7. If you *presume* something, you _____.
   (A) question it very seriously
   (B) see it before anyone else
   (C) believe it to be true
   (D) deny its existence

   7. _____

8. A *presumption* can best be described as _____.
   (A) a question raised for no apparent reason or purpose
   (B) vigorous denial of guilt
   (C) the belief that something is true without having proof
   (D) something that stands in the way of learning the truth

   8. _____

When the store ran out of the items on sale, the manager gave each customer a coupon that could be *redeemed* for that item at a later date. *Redemption* had to be made within 30 days.

9. To *redeem* is to _____.
   (A) turn in or exchange
   (B) increase the price
   (C) refuse to accept
   (D) place in danger

   9. _____

10. *Redemption* is best defined as _____.
    (A) a loss that cannot be replaced
    (B) the recovery of something given up or lost
    (C) an illegal attempt to cheat someone
    (D) something used in place of money

    10. _____

136 Related Words

Name _____

Lesson 30 Part B

Applying Meaning

Read each sentence below. Write "correct" on the answer line if the vocabulary word has been used correctly or "incorrect" if it has been used incorrectly.

1. In our legal system, a person accused of a crime is *consumed* to be innocent until proven guilty.

1. _____

2. In order to *redeem* his watch from the pawn shop, Jack had to present his ticket and make a payment of $50.

2. _____

3. After pleading for an hour to let me see the movie, I began to *perceive* a slight change in my mother's attitude.

3. _____

4. Deciding whether or not to attend college is one of the most important *deceptions* a young person must make.

4. _____

5. When the electrical system broke down at half-time, the *presumption* of the game was delayed for nearly an hour.

5. _____

For each word used incorrectly, write a sentence using the word properly.

_____
_____
_____
_____
_____
_____
_____

Follow the directions below to write a sentence using a vocabulary word.

6. Use *consumption* in a sentence about a town's drinking water after a flood.

_____
_____
_____

7. Write a sentence about coupons at a grocery store. Use the word *redemption*.

_____
_____
_____

Related Words 137

8. Use any form of the word *perception* in a sentence about one or more people observing an event.

   _____
   _____
   _____

9. Write a sentence about an important event. Use any form of the word *presume*.

   _____
   _____
   _____

10. Use any form of the word *deceive* in a sentence about an advertisement.

    _____
    _____
    _____

Test-Taking Strategies

Tests of reading comprehension ask you to read one or two selections and answer some questions to test how well you understood what you read. The questions often ask you to draw inferences from the information. For example, if someone is shivering and rubbing his hands, you would be expected to infer that he is cold.

Practice: Reread the selection "The Ancient Civilization of the Maya" on page 57. Write an X next to each statement that can be inferred from this essay.

1. The Mayan people arrived in southern Mexico and Central America by boat.   1. _____

2. The powerful Mayan families paid artists to create their art and architecture.   2. _____

3. Until the discovery of the Mayan calendar, the Christian calendar was thought to be the most advanced one of the time.   3. _____

4. The Maya were strong and athletic.   4. _____

5. Contact with the outside world hastened the fall of the Mayan civilization.   5. _____

Assessment

Name _____

How well do you remember the words you studied in Lessons 28–30? Take the following test covering the words from the last three lessons.

Part 1 Choose the Correct Meaning

Each question below includes a word in capital letters, followed by four words or phrases. Choose the word or phrase that is <u>closest</u> in meaning to the words in capital letters. Write the letter for your answer on the line provided.

Sample

S. FINISH	(A) enjoy	(B) complete	S. __**B**__
	(C) destroy	(D) enlarge	

1. ASPECT	(A) appeal	(B) summary	1. _____
	(C) point of view	(D) question	
2. YARN	(A) lost treasure	(B) a tale	2. _____
	(C) a play	(D) new idea	
3. SINISTER	(A) simple	(B) evil	3. _____
	(C) familiar	(D) unusual	
4. SCUTTLE	(A) rescue	(B) weigh	4. _____
	(C) paint	(D) sink	
5. WINDWARD	(A) direction from which the wind blows	(B) direction toward which the wind blows	5. _____
	(C) drafty	(D) the northeast	
6. CONSUMPTION	(A) careful preparations	(B) type of seasoning	6. _____
	(C) storage area	(D) the act of using up	
7. NEBULOUS	(A) harmless	(B) hazy	7. _____
	(C) very old	(D) smooth	
8. EVOKE	(A) take back	(B) stand tall	8. _____
	(C) forget	(D) stir up	
9. AGGRESSOR	(A) winner	(B) attacker	9. _____
	(C) soldier	(D) leader	
10. ESTEEM	(A) request	(B) desire	10. _____
	(C) regard	(D) guess	

11. CAPSIZE (A) tip over (B) reduce 11. _____
(C) change course (D) slow down

12. KNOT (A) unit of time (B) unit of money 12. _____
(C) unit of speed (D) unit of strength

13. PRESUME (A) suppose (B) hear 13. _____
(C) assign (D) record

14. BALLAST (A) safety equipment (B) explosion 14. _____
(C) training guides (D) weight

15. REDEEM (A) sort out (B) think over 15. _____
(C) turn in (D) take back

Part 2 Matching Words and Meaning

Match the definition in Column B with the word in Column A. Write the letter of the correct definition on the line provided.

Column A **Column B**

16. bow   a. the right side of a ship   16. _____
17. perception   b. trick   17. _____
18. anonymous   c. the front of a ship   18. _____
19. consume   d. to cause or bring about   19. _____
20. starboard   e. understanding   20. _____
21. provoke   f. unnamed   21. _____
22. deception   g. eat   22. _____
23. stern   h. the back of a ship   23. _____
24. shoal   i. variety   24. _____
25. assortment   j. shallow area of water   25. _____

Context Clues: Social Studies

Lesson 31 Part A

Name _____

The 19th Amendment

"The right of the citizens of the United States to vote shall not be denied or abridged by the United States or any State on account of sex." This hardly sounds like a **radical** idea. Could any reasonable person **dispute** the fairness of such a statement? It may be unthinkable now, but less than a hundred years ago, this **proposition** was the subject of heated discussion.

Even in the 19th century, women had few rights. Men ran their families and the government. Only men could buy and sell property. If they went to school at all, women were given only a basic education. The marriage vows required a woman to "love, honor, and obey" her husband, and the right to vote was limited to men.

Change was painfully slow, but it finally came. The **unwavering** dedication of women like Elizabeth Stanton, Lucretia Mott, and Susan B. Anthony helped to **motivate** all women to seek justice. At an 1848 meeting held in Seneca Falls, New York, 68 women and 32 men signed a statement demanding women be given equality with men. Still, getting the right to vote proved a **daunting** task. When they were allowed to speak in public, women were frequently exposed to **derisive** shouts from the audience. Newspapers and some churches **reprimanded** them for seeking to change the "natural order of things." Even women slammed doors in the faces of those **circulating** petitions. Then the Civil War broke out, and the movement slowed to a near halt.

A surprising event occurred after the war. The Wyoming Territory, where men outnumbered women by almost ten to one, granted women the right to vote. Some believe it was a **stratagem** to attract more women to the area, but whatever the reason, by 1896 three western states had followed Wyoming's example. By 1917 sixteen states had granted women the right to vote, but things seemed to stop there. A constitutional amendment was the only way to guarantee all women the right to vote.

Such an amendment had been proposed for some 40 years, but it had never passed. In spite of an overwhelming number of petitions, it was defeated again in 1914. After President Wilson gave his support, the amendment was finally passed and sent to the states for approval in 1919. With Tennessee's approval in 1920 the 19th Amendment became the law of the land.

Words
- circulate
- daunting
- derisive
- dispute
- motivate
- proposition
- radical
- reprimand
- stratagem
- unwavering

Each word in this lesson's word list appears in dark type in the selection you just read. Think about how the vocabulary word is used in the selection; then write the letter for the best answer to each question.

1. Another word for *radical* (line 3) is _____.
   (A) extreme   (B) friendly
   (C) useless   (D) patriotic

   1. _____

2. If you *dispute* (line 4) something, you _____.
   (A) divide it into parts   (B) agree with it
   (C) sent it away   (D) argue over it

   2. _____

3. A *proposition* (line 5) can best be described as a _____.
   (A) religious belief   (B) pleasant exchange of ideas
   (C) proposal or offer (D) prediction

   3. _____

4. If one's dedication is *unwavering* (line 12), it _____.
   (A) changes with the times   (B) never changes or hesitates
   (C) is hidden from others   (D) is difficult to explain

   4. _____

5. To *motivate* (line 14) is to _____.
   (A) move others to take action   (B) deny the rights of others
   (C) excuse the need for   (D) explain away

   5. _____

6. A *daunting* (line 17) task is _____.
   (A) simple   (B) amusing
   (C) impossible   (D) discouraging

   6. _____

7. A *derisive* (line 19) shout is one that _____.
   (A) encourages   (B) is barely heard
   (C) is ignored   (D) mocks or ridicules

   7. _____

8. To *reprimand* (line 20) is to _____.
   (A) praise   (B) scold harshly
   (C) bless   (D) decline

   8. _____

9. If you are *circulating* (line 22) a petition, you are _____.
   (A) distributing it   (B) destroying it
   (C) planning it   (D) ignoring it

   9. _____

10. A *stratagem* (line 26) is a(n) _____.
    (A) long speech   (B) clever plan or trick
    (C) area of land (D) tight fitting garment

    10. _____

142   Context Clues: Social Studies

Name _____

Lesson 31 Part B

Applying Meaning

Decide which word in parentheses best completes the sentence. Then write the sentence, adding the missing word.

1. To many of the Southern colonists, seeking independence from England was too _____ to be taken seriously. (derisive; radical)

   _____
   _____
   _____

2. The store offered to pay students $10 per hour to _____ among the shoppers in the mall and give away discount coupons. (circulate; motivate)

   _____
   _____
   _____

3. My father's _____ was quite simple and direct; if I washed and waxed the car, he would take me to the movies. (proposition; stratagem)

   _____
   _____
   _____

4. The officer could have given Cali a ticket for speeding but instead decided to _____ her. (dispute; reprimand)

   _____
   _____
   _____

5. I avoided the _____ chore of writing the report on our field trip as long as possible. (daunting; derisive)

   _____
   _____
   _____

Each question below contains a vocabulary word from this lesson. Answer each question "yes" or "no" in the space provided.

6. Does a good football coach try to *motivate* his team during halftime?   6. _____

Context Clues: Social Studies   143

7. Is it wise for a baseball player to make *derisive* comments to the umpire?

7. _____

8. Does an army officer want the *unwavering* loyalty of the men and women in his unit when he leads them into a dangerous battle?

8. _____

9. Do responsible industries *dispute* of any dangerous pollutants in a proper manner?

9. _____

10. If you were stranded on an island, would you welcome a *stratagem* for being rescued?

10. _____

For each question you answered "no," write a sentence explaining your answer.

_____
_____
_____
_____
_____
_____
_____

Mastering Meaning

Of all the world's democracies, the United States has one of the poorest voter turnouts for elections. In many cases, fewer than half of all eligible voters actually take the time to cast a vote. Write an essay explaining what you think are the reasons for this poor turnout and what you would do to increase it. Use some of the words you studied in this lesson.

Vocabulary from French

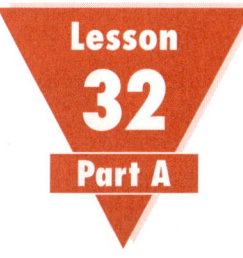

Name _____

You may have heard a foreign visitor struggle to express a word or idea in English. Often the problem is not a lack of knowledge of English, but the fact that English does not have a word that matches a word from that person's language. Often the solution is to use the word from the other language as though it were an English word. After a while, some words are so commonly used that we forget the foreign source. In this lesson you will study 10 words that came into English from the French language because we needed a word for something.

Unlocking Meaning

Read the sentences or short passages below. Write the letter for the correct definition of the italicized vocabulary word.

Words
- antique
- avalanche
- barricade
- casserole
- collage
- curfew
- debris
- envoy
- procedure
- vague

1. This valuable *antique* chair was made in Boston in the 18th century from oak and pine. It is believed that Paul Revere owned it at one time.
   - (A) damaged
   - (B) belonging to an earlier time
   - (C) well constructed
   - (D) expensive

2. The decision to drop football from the program of extracurricular activities caused an *avalanche* of protests from angry parents and students.
   - (A) huge or overwhelming amount
   - (B) small number
   - (C) well packaged
   - (D) carefully worded

3. The excited crowd was warned to stay behind the *barricade* and off the playing field at the conclusion of the game.
   - (A) a large wooden container
   - (B) equipment used in a sport such as baseball
   - (C) a law designed to protect property
   - (D) a structure intended to block one's way

4. Morrie carefully placed the macaroni and cheese *casserole* on a pad on the middle of the table. We had to wait 10 minutes before it was cool enough to serve.
   - (A) type of dessert
   - (B) any food that is easily prepared
   - (C) food baked and served in the same dish
   - (D) dairy products

1. _____

2. _____

3. _____

4. _____

Vocabulary from French   145

5. In art class we used old photographs, a broken pen, notebook paper, and part of an old bulletin board to make a *collage* about our school.
   (A) utensil found in most kitchens
   (B) exact copy
   (C) system used to repair badly broken items
   (D) art made by gluing articles on a surface

5. _____

6. The coach placed a 10 o'clock *curfew* on all team members the night before a game. She wanted her team to be well rested when it took the field.
   (A) rule requiring people to be indoors by a certain time
   (B) meeting called in addition to regularly scheduled meetings
   (C) treatment for injuries suffered in sports
   (D) a plan to surprise an opponent

6. _____

7. The force of the powerful tornado destroyed scores of homes and left *debris* scattered over a 10-mile area.
   (A) cost of repairing damage
   (B) the remains of something broken
   (C) a method of forecasting storms
   (D) large, flat surface

7. _____

8. The United States sent an *envoy* to several European countries to ask for their support in the dispute with Iraq.
   (A) formal treaty
   (B) challenge
   (C) government representative
   (D) someone famous for his or her scientific knowledge

8. _____

9. Drivers wishing to renew their licenses must follow a certain *procedure*. First they must pass an eye test. Then they will have their picture taken. Finally they must sign the license.
   (A) difficult assignment
   (B) way of doing something
   (C) confusing instruction
   (D) special permission to do something

9. _____

10. To avoid taking a stand on the important, but difficult, issue, the senator gave *vague* answers to questions about his position. No one knew exactly how he would vote on the bill.
    (A) lengthy
    (B) precise
    (C) popular
    (D) unclear

10. _____

Vocabulary from French

Name _____

Applying Meaning

Decide which word in parentheses best completes the sentence. Then write the sentence, adding the missing word.

1. As part of the city beautification project, residents were asked to remove litter and _____ from the roadsides and vacant lots. (barricades; debris)

   _____
   _____
   _____

2. In the distance we could see the _____ outline of a ship approaching through the mist. (antique; vague)

   _____
   _____
   _____

3. The star player on our basketball team has received a(n) _____ of scholarship offers from various colleges. (avalanche; collage)

   _____
   _____
   _____

4. Grandma recalls playing with some of the _____ toys we saw in the shop. (antique; vague)

   _____
   _____
   _____

5. Although he preferred working with watercolors or clay, the artist occasionally created extremely interesting _____. (casseroles; collages)

   _____
   _____
   _____

Each question below contains a vocabulary word from this lesson. Answer each question "yes" or "no" in the space provided.

6. Are *casseroles* attached to the bottom of furniture in order to make them easier to move about a room?   6. _____

Vocabulary from French

7. Would you expect to find *barricades* along the side of a parade route?

7. _____

8. In a fairy tale, is it common to read about evil witches placing a *curfew* on someone?

8. _____

9. Do librarians establish a certain *procedure* for checking out a book?

9. _____

10. Might a poor person *envoy* the things a wealthy person possesses?

10. _____

For each question you answered "no," write a sentence explaining your answer.

_____
_____
_____
_____
_____
_____
_____
_____

Bonus Words

French is just one language from which English has borrowed. In fact, few languages have escaped the English language's appetite for new words.

Match the Word and Its Source: Try guessing the origin of some common English words. Match each word in the Word list with a country from the Source list. Then check your answer in a dictionary.

Word		Source	
ghoul	khaki	Spanish	Arabic
omelet	taboo	Bantu	Italian
stampede	kayak	Persian	Eskimo
spaghetti	gumbo	French	Polynesian

The Roots -pen- and -port-

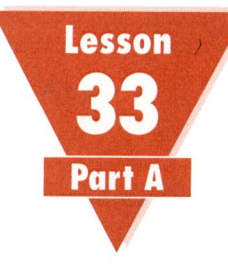

Lesson 33 Part A

Name _____

The Latin word *pendere* means "to weigh," "to pay," or "to hang." It appears in English words as the root *-pen-* or *-pend-*. The *-port-* root found in many English words comes from the Latin word *portare*, meaning "to carry." The original Latin meanings may have changed somewhat in modern English words, but there is usually a hint of the original meaning. If you support a person, you may "carry" him through a difficult period. If you depend on someone, you "hang" on to her for help.

Root	Meaning	English Word
-pen-	weigh, hang, pay	appendix
-pend-	weigh, hang, pay	dependent
-port-	carry	porter

Words
- appendix
- dependable
- dependent
- expenditure
- passport
- pendulum
- pension
- porter
- supportive
- suspend

Unlocking Meaning

A vocabulary word appears in italics in each sentence or short passage below. Find the root in the vocabulary word and think about how the word is used in the passage. Then write a definition for the vocabulary word. Compare your definition with the one in the dictionary at the back of the book.

1. The contract explained the duties of the repair crew and the amount of their payment, but the detailed schedule for completing the work appeared in an *appendix* attached to the agreement.

   _____
   _____
   _____

2. The newspapers in colonial America were not always a *dependable* source of facts. Publishers tended to make the facts fit their point of view.

   _____
   _____
   _____

3. Coach O'Toole felt that the outcome of the game would be *dependent* on the physical condition of the players.

   _____
   _____
   _____

The Roots -pen- and -port- 149

4. My congresswoman was firmly against any government *expenditure* that would lead to an increase in taxes.

5. The college claimed that its courses in business and sales were a *passport* to success and great wealth.

6. In one short story, a man is tied beneath a razor-sharp *pendulum* that slowly lowers as it swings back and forth.

7. For years, Emilio contributed money to his retirement fund. Last year he was able to quit work and collect a monthly *pension*.

8. Aunt Meg had so much luggage that she had to have a *porter* help her get everything from the baggage area to her car.

9. Although Myra's father did not like her idea of joining the Marine Corps, he promised to be *supportive* of her decision.

10. After the mysterious crash of the new plane, the government decided to *suspend* all future flights until it found the cause of the accident.

Name _____

Lesson 33 Part B

Applying Meaning

Decide which word in parentheses best completes the sentence. Then write the sentence, adding the missing word.

1. The lion was raised at the zoo and had become _____ on his keepers for food. (dependent; supportive)

2. The manager refused to approve any new _____ for furniture or equipment until sales of the company's products improved. (expenditures; pensions)

3. With each swing of the clock's _____, the time for our departure drew nearer. (appendix; pendulum)

4. The workers feared that the company's collapse would endanger their _____. (expenditures; pensions)

5. The early settlers chose to locate their village near a _____ source of water and firewood. (dependable; supportive)

The Roots -pen- and -port-

Follow the directions below to write a sentence using a vocabulary word.

6. Use any form of *suspend* in a sentence about school.

   _____
   _____
   _____

7. Describe a scene at a hotel using any form of the word *porter*.

   _____
   _____
   _____

8. Tell about a book you read or plan to read. Use the word *appendix*.

   _____
   _____
   _____

9. Use *passport* in a sentence about a turning point in someone's life.

   _____
   _____
   _____

10. Use *supportive* to describe what someone has done for you.

    _____
    _____
    _____

Bonus Words

Sometimes a person becomes so closely associated with an action or thing that his or her name takes on a new meaning. For example, James Brudenell, the Seventh Earl of Cardigan, was famous for his elegant dress. One item he favored was a type of sweater. Today a collarless, buttoned sweater is called a cardigan.

Define the "People" Words: Use a dictionary or encyclopedia to find out about the person behind these words. Report your findings to the class.

boysenberry   Braille   Stetson

spoonerism   platonic   guppy

Assessment

Name _____

How well do you remember the words you studied in Lessons 31–33? Take the following test covering the words from the last three lessons.

Part 1 Antonyms

Each question below includes a word in capital letters, followed by four words or phrases. Choose the word or phrase that is most nearly <u>opposite</u> in meaning to the word in capital letters. Consider all choices before deciding on your answer. Write the letter for your answer on the line provided.

Sample

S. SLOW	(A) lazy	(B) fast	S. ____B____
	(C) simple	(D) common	
1. ANTIQUE	(A) modern	(B) worthless	1. _____
	(C) pretty	(D) old	
2. UNWAVERING	(A) thoughtful	(B) surprising	2. _____
	(C) changeable	(D) colorful	
3. PASSPORT	(A) sluggish	(B) exception	3. _____
	(C) barrier	(D) citizen	
4. VAGUE	(A) loud	(B) clear	4. _____
	(C) usual	(D) unique	
5. RADICAL	(A) popular	(B) cautious	5. _____
	(C) scary	(D) new	
6. REPRIMAND	(A) report	(B) question	6. _____
	(C) command	(D) praise	
7. DEPENDENT	(A) along with	(B) free from	7. _____
	(C) instead of	(D) in addition to	
8. SUSPEND	(A) extend	(B) record	8. _____
	(C) suggest	(D) discuss	
9. DERISIVE	(A) spoiled	(B) complimentary	9. _____
	(C) famous	(D) tempting	
10. MOTIVATE	(A) teach	(B) challenge	10. _____
	(C) require	(D) discourage	

Assessment 153

11. CIRCULATE   (A) hold back   (B) deliver   11. _____
                   (C) move   (D) hide

12. DEPENDABLE   (A) friendly   (B) dishonorable   12. _____
                   (C) unreliable   (D) knowledgeable

13. DAUNTING   (A) long   (B) encouraging   13. _____
                   (C) difficult   (D) simple

14. SUPPORTIVE   (A) hostile   (B) hard working   14. _____
                   (C) clearheaded   (D) wealthy

15. DISPUTE   (A) disprove   (B) share   15. _____
                   (C) question   (D) agree

Part 2 Matching Words and Meaning

Match the definition in Column B with the word in Column A. Write the letter of the correct definition on the line provided.

Column A   **Column B**

16. casserole   a. proposal   16. _____
17. porter   b. government representative   17. _____
18. envoy   c. retirement income   18. _____
19. appendix   d. food baked in one dish   19. _____
20. procedure   e. money spent   20. _____
21. proposition   f. method for doing   21. _____
22. pension   g. time to be in   22. _____
23. stratagem   h. person who carries baggage   23. _____
24. curfew   i. plan or trick   24. _____
25. expenditure   j. part of a book   25. _____

Context Clues: The Sciences

Name _____

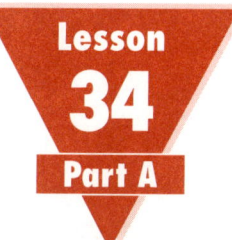

The Rocket's Red Glare

In the 17th century, Sir Isaac Newton published his Third Law: For every action there is an equal and opposite reaction. If you have ever rowed a boat across a quiet lake, you experienced Newton's law in action. The action of pushing the oars in one direction pro-
5 pelled the boat in the opposite direction. This simple rule of nature is the basis for the rockets that **catapult** both bombs and people into the air.

The first mention of rockets appeared in various Chinese writings of the 13th century. Several writers report rockets being used
10 to drive off Mongol invaders. Why rockets were invented in China is anyone's guess. Some historians **surmise** that the high levels of sulfur and potassium nitrate in the soil may have been accidentally kicked into a campfire, resulting in an explosion. The **transition** from explosion to rocketry required an additional step. When this
15 explosion is created in a hollow tube that is capped on one end, the force of the explosion is **vented** through a single opening. This "action" in one direction, moves the tube in an "equal and opposite" direction. The force of the **discharge** can be increased or decreased by widening or narrowing the opening. This principle can
20 be demonstrated with a garden hose. The smaller the opening, the greater the force of the escaping water.

As with the 13th century Chinese, the first **application** of this technology in Europe was in weaponry. The ability to send balls of fire at a distant enemy offered a clear advantage in battle. The prob-
25 lem was accuracy. On land, the cannon provided greater **leverage** for an army because its aim was more precise and its performance more reliable. Moreover, the equipment required for launching rockets proved too **cumbersome** to move and set up under fire or in bad weather. However, it was at sea that the rocket proved itself
30 to be a **practical** and effective weapon. The huge canvas sails and tarred hull of an enemy ship offered a perfect target. A single rocket could **engulf** a ship in flames in a matter of minutes.

As the accuracy of rockets increased, they began to play a part in ground warfare. The V-1 and V-2 rockets developed by the
35 Germans in World War II terrified London. Today's intercontinental missiles with their atomic warheads are some of the most feared weapons in history.

More recently, people have replaced warheads, and the rocket has become the preferred method of space travel.

Words
- application
- catapult
- cumbersome
- discharge
- engulf
- leverage
- practical
- surmise
- transition
- vent

Unlocking Meaning

Each word in this lesson's word list appears in dark type in the selection you just read. Think about how the vocabulary word is used in the selection; then write the letter for the best answer to each question.

1. Another word for *catapult* (line 6) is _____.
   - (A) prevent
   - (B) destroy
   - (C) dismiss
   - (D) hurl

   1. _____

2. If you *surmise* (line 11) something, you _____.
   - (A) suppose it to be true
   - (B) strongly deny it
   - (C) reduce its size
   - (D) plan it carefully

   2. _____

3. A *transition* (line 13) is the _____.
   - (A) ability to see through something
   - (B) passing from one thing to another
   - (C) work done by a scientist
   - (D) end of a rocket

   3. _____

4. To *vent* (line 16) is to _____.
   - (A) prove
   - (B) divide
   - (C) release
   - (D) seal

   4. _____

5. A *discharge* (line 18) can best be described as a(n) _____.
   - (A) unfortunate accident
   - (B) type of weapon
   - (C) sudden release
   - (D) law of nature

   5. _____

6. Another word for *application* (line 22) is _____.
   - (A) use
   - (B) theft
   - (C) description
   - (D) disaster

   6. _____

7. Another word for *leverage* (line 25) is _____.
   - (A) movement
   - (B) fame
   - (C) shelter
   - (D) advantage

   7. _____

8. If something is *cumbersome* (line 28), it is _____.
   - (A) pleasant
   - (B) awkward
   - (C) simple
   - (D) unfamiliar

   8. _____

9. Another word for *practical* (line 30), is _____.
   - (A) workable
   - (B) skillful
   - (C) movable
   - (D) unreliable

   9. _____

10. To *engulf* (line 32) is to _____.
    - (A) remove
    - (B) raise up
    - (C) swallow up
    - (D) enjoy

    10. _____

156   Context Clues: The Sciences

Name _____

Lesson 34 Part B

Applying Meaning

Decide which word in parentheses best completes the sentence. Then write the sentence, adding the missing word.

1. The frown on Ms. Kinel's face as she returned my homework made me _____ that I had not done it correctly. (surmise; vent)

2. It took four people to finish the _____ task of getting the new refrigerator up the stairs. (cumbersome; practical)

3. The advertisement claimed that this quick-drying glue had hundreds of _____ around the house. (applications; transitions)

4. By cutting off all sources of supply, Grant gained the _____ he needed to demand the surrender of Vicksburg. (application; leverage)

5. Unable to turn sharply at such a high speed, the skier was _____ into a pile of snow. (catapulted; engulfed)

Read each sentence or short passage below. Write "correct" on the answer line if the vocabulary word has been used correctly or "incorrect" if it has been used incorrectly.

6. The accident victim had lost a great deal of blood, so the doctor ordered that he be given a *transition* immediately.

6. _____

Context Clues: The Sciences

7. The huge explosion rocked several communities. The *discharge* could be felt as far as 30 miles away.

7. _____

8. Before breaking ground for the new office building, it was necessary to *engulf* the services of an architect.

8. _____

9. The law forbids boaters to *vent* their fuel or untreated waste into the water.

9. _____

10. All students were required to get some *practical* experience on the job before they could receive a diploma.

10. _____

For each word used incorrectly, write a sentence using the word properly.

_____
_____
_____
_____
_____
_____
_____
_____
_____
_____

Mastering Meaning

Rockets have revolutionized warfare and the exploration of space. What other inventions of the past 100 years do you feel have had a major effect on the way we live? There have been important medical, electronic, and mechanical breakthroughs in recent years. Write a short essay explaining your choice of the most important invention in the past 100 years. Use some of the words you studied in this lesson.

Vocabulary of Literature

Lesson 35 Part A

Name _____

Just as engineers and doctors have words to describe their particular world of work, writers and readers of literature have special words to describe elements unique to their field. It would be difficult to discuss poetry or fiction without using terms that describe how words are used or an that explain an author's technique. In this lesson you will learn 10 words frequently used in writing or talking about literature. You may have already used some in class.

Unlocking Meaning

Words
- alliteration
- ballad
- couplet
- imagery
- lyric poem
- meter
- realism
- rhyme
- satire
- verse

Read the sentences or short passages below. Write the letter for the correct definition of the italicized vocabulary word.

1. Poe's mastery of *alliteration* can be seen in the third stanza of "The Raven," with the phrase "The silken, sad uncertain rustling of each purple curtain . . ."
   - (A) lack of meaning
   - (B) the repetition of a sound
   - (C) humor
   - (D) exaggeration

2. Their gentle notes and fascinating stories of adventure or romance made *ballads* a popular form of courtly entertainment in medieval England.
   - (A) the story of a famous person's life
   - (B) religious argument
   - (C) a song-like poem
   - (D) a short work of fiction

3. The first scene in *Macbeth* ends with the famous *couplet*
   "Fair is foul, and foul is fair.
   Hover through the fog and filthy air."
   - (A) story involving imaginary characters
   - (B) early form of drama
   - (C) confusing comparison
   - (D) pair of lines ending with the same sound

4. When Sandburg says that fog comes "on little cat feet," he is using the *imagery* of a cat to suggest the quiet softness of fog.
   - (A) descriptive language or comparison
   - (B) reference to the Bible
   - (C) sad event
   - (D) unexpected actions

1. _____

2. _____

3. _____

4. _____

Vocabulary of Literature 159

5. Because of the importance they placed on the emotions, the Romantic poets produced many *lyric poems*.
   (A) play in three acts
   (B) short horror story
   (C) type of literature that expresses the emotions of the speaker
   (D) volume of poetry written by a modern writer

5. _____

6. To help her students hear the *meter*, the teacher had them clap their hands with every beat as she read the poem aloud.
   (A) quiet mood
   (B) pattern of stress or beats
   (C) conversation between two people
   (D) unusual comparison

6. _____

7. The shocking *realism* in some movies has caused some groups to call for warnings to be printed in all ads for movies containing violent scenes.
   (A) creative presentation
   (B) falsehood
   (C) example
   (D) presenting things as they actually are

7. _____

8. The words "seen" and "green" *rhyme*.
   (A) have similar meanings
   (B) end with the same sounds
   (C) have opposite meanings
   (D) are never used together

8. _____

9. Swift's "Modest Proposal" is a bitter *satire* in which he seems to seriously suggest eating children to solve the food shortage.
   (A) writing that ridicules human shortcomings
   (B) love poem
   (C) story intended to amuse children
   (D) song about knights and chivalry

9. _____

10. Frost's "Stopping By Woods on a Snowy Evening" contains 16 lines. Each of its four *verses* contains four lines.
    (A) long lines
    (B) poetry about the seasons
    (C) parts of a longer poem
    (D) poem of unknown authorship

10. _____

160 Vocabulary of Literature

Name _____

Lesson 35 Part B

Applying Meaning

Write the vocabulary word that fits each clue below. Then write a sentence using the vocabulary word correctly.

1. It is another word for rhythm.
   _____
   _____
   _____

2. It is the opposite of make-believe.
   _____
   _____
   _____

3. These words are an example: pity, city, kitty.
   _____
   _____
   _____

4. You might write one of these to express your dislike for someone's actions or behavior.
   _____
   _____
   _____

5. You might strum a guitar and recite one about one of your personal heroes.
   _____
   _____
   _____

6. It is heard in this line: "A fair field full of folk . . ."
   _____
   _____
   _____

Vocabulary of Literature

Decide which word in parentheses best completes the sentence. Then write the sentence, adding the missing word.

7. The first _____ of Robert Browning's 36-line poem, "Confession," contains two questions and an answer. (satire; verse)

   _____

   _____

   _____

8. I wanted to end my poem with a _____, but I could not think of a word that ended like *balloon*. (couplet; meter)

   _____

   _____

   _____

9. The _____ in many Romantic poems involves a comparison between people and the natural world. (imagery; meter)

   _____

   _____

   _____

10. The _____ of Elizabeth Barrett Browning frequently expressed her deep love and affection for her husband. (lyric poems; satire)

    _____

    _____

    _____

Our Living Language

Hackney, a suburb of London, England, was a place where people rented horses and carriages for dull, repetitious work. These came to be known as *hacks*, a shortened form of *Hackney*. The word *hackney* lives on as a term to describe anything that has become trite or dull through overuse. A hackneyed expression is one that may have been clever at one time but has been repeated so often that it is meaningless.

Make a List: List some hackneyed expressions that you hear often. Compare your list with those of your classmates. Did you identify many of the same expressions?

The Root -ject-

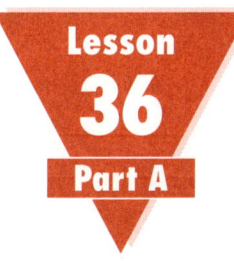

Lesson 36 Part A

Name _____

The *-ject-* root seen in many English words comes from the Latin word *jacere*, meaning "to throw." Some words with the *-ject-* root still have a suggestion of throwing in their meanings. Sometimes the root is spelled *jet*, but usually you will see *ject* in words with this root.

Root	Meaning	English Word
-ject-	to throw	reject
-jet-	to throw	jettison

Unlocking Meaning

Words
- dejection
- eject
- inject
- jettison
- objection
- projectile
- projection
- reject
- subject
- trajectory

A vocabulary word appears in italics in each sentence or short passage below. Find the root in the vocabulary word and think about how it is used in the passage. Then write a definition for the vocabulary word. Compare your definition with the one in the dictionary at the back of the book.

1. After losing by just two points, the team slowly made its way to the lockers. *Dejection* could be seen in each player's face.

   _____
   _____
   _____

2. The principal announced that he would *eject* rowdy students from the assembly and send them directly home.

   _____
   _____
   _____

3. The nurse patiently explained why it was necessary to *inject* the vaccine into my thigh.

   _____
   _____
   _____

4. The huge gun could fire a 100-pound *projectile*.

   _____
   _____
   _____

5. The only *objection* to building the playground came from neighbors who felt it would cause traffic safety problems.

6. Before taking off from the moon's surface, the astronauts had to *jettison* all unnecessary equipment. The lighter the load, the less fuel they would need.

7. Under the microscope we could see the small *projection* the insect uses to sting its victims.

8. The workers voted to *reject* management's offer because the pay increase was less than they had asked for.

9. Maveed's attempt to *subject* his new puppy to his rules was not very successful.

10. The rocket's fiery exhaust allowed us to follow its *trajectory* through the night sky.

Name _____

Lesson 36 Part B

Applying Meaning

Decide which word in parentheses best completes the sentence. Then write the sentence, adding the missing word.

1. As she squeezed through the small door of the cabin, Helen caught her sweater on a small _____. (projectile; projection)

2. Since no _____ was made to the planned celebration, the mayor appointed a committee to begin work. (objection; trajectory)

3. The scientist _____ a red dye into the animal tissue so it would be easier to see under the microscope. (injected; subjected)

4. Fearing that his fuel tanks would explode in a crash, the pilot of the disabled plane decided to _____ them over the desert. (jettison; reject)

5. For security reasons, anyone applying for a government job will be _____ to a thorough examination of his or her background. (ejected; subjected)

Read each sentence below. Write "correct" on the answer line if the vocabulary word has been used correctly or "incorrect" if it has been used incorrectly.

6. The general ordered all officers to assemble in the *trajectory* at 8:00 A.M.

6. _____

7. Ed chose to *reject* the advice of his doctor and make the trip to Mexico.

7. _____

8. The umpire warned that any players involved in a fight risked immediate *dejection* from the game.

8. _____

9. The workers covered the walls of the kitchen with *projectiles* of various colors and styles.

9. _____

10. When the computer is turned off, it automatically *ejects* any disks in its drive.

10. _____

Test-Taking Strategies

Some standardized tests ask you to select the best word or words to complete a sentence. These tests require a combination of vocabulary and reasoning skills. Before selecting an answer, read each item carefully and eliminate the choices that are obviously incorrect. Then search for clues to the overall meaning of the sentence. Finally, try each of the possible answers in the sentence and choose the best one.

Practice: Choose the word or set of words that, when used in the sentence, best fits its meaning.

1. After standing in line for hours to get tickets, we were _____ to learn that all tickets had been sold when we reached the booth.
   (A) excited   (B) disappointed
   (C) amused   (D) ashamed

1. _____

2. Most of the cars we saw at the auto show were _____; some were from Europe, but most came from Japan and Korea.
   (A) damaged   (B) small
   (C) foreign   (D) expensive

2. _____

3. Jeff was anxious to _____ his homework so he could attend the game on Sunday.
   (A) ignore   (B) correct
   (C) deliver   (D) complete

3. _____

4. Although the reviews of the film were _____, the movie was actually quite _____.
   (A) positive . . . boring   (B) long . . . good
   (C) unknown . . . interesting (D) simple . . . crowded

4. _____

166   The Root *-ject-*

Assessment

Lessons 34-36

Name _____

How well do you remember the words you studied in Lessons 30–36? Take the following test covering the words from the last three lessons.

Part 1 Choose the Correct Meaning

Each question below includes a word in capital letters, followed by four words or phrases. Choose the word or phrase that is <u>closest</u> in meaning to the word in capital letters. Write the letter for your answer on the line provided

Sample

| S. FINISH | (A) enjoy | (B) complete | S. ____B____ |
| | (C) destroy | (D) enlarge | |

| 1. SATIRE | (A) path of flight | (B) ridicule | 1. _____ |
| | (C) clothing | (D) bitter | |

| 2. APPLICATION | (A) use | (B) request | 2. _____ |
| | (C) decoration | (D) payment | |

| 3. METER | (A) case | (B) matter | 3. _____ |
| | (C) rhythm | (D) explanation | |

| 4. EJECT | (A) divide | (B) throw out | 4. _____ |
| | (C) present | (D) warn | |

| 5. DISCHARGE | (A) attack | (B) payment | 5. _____ |
| | (C) prevention | (D) forceful release | |

| 6. ALLITERATION | (A) same first sound | (B) carefully worded | 6. _____ |
| | (C) comparison | (D) part of a poem | |

| 7. PROJECTILE | (A) building material | (B) hurled body | 7. _____ |
| | (C) small project | (D) cage | |

| 8. JETTISON | (A) turn around | (B) type of engine | 8. _____ |
| | (C) throw away | (D) narrow tube | |

| 9. DEJECTION | (A) blemish | (B) threat | 9. _____ |
| | (C) command | (D) discouragement | |

| 10. SUBJECT | (A) praise | (B) raise | 10. _____ |
| | (C) name | (D) bring under control | |

| 11. IMAGERY | (A) word picture | (B) imaginary | 11. _____ |
| | (C) exclamation | (D) suggestion | |

Assessment 167

12. TRANSITION	(A) vision	(B) entrance	12. _____
	(C) passage	(D) position	
13. CATAPULT	(A) arrange into groups	(B) shoot	13. _____
	(C) similar word	(D) handle	
14. ENGULF	(A) overwhelm	(B) hold under water	14. _____
	(C) compete	(D) even out	
15. INJECT	(A) withdraw	(B) place in danger	15. _____
	(C) question	(D) insert	

Part 2 Matching Words and Meaning

Match the definition in Column B with the word in Column A. Write the letter of the correct definition on the line provided.

Column A	Column B	
16. ballad	a. path	16. _____
17. leverage	b. awkward	17. _____
18. trajectory	c. true presentation	18. _____
19. projection	d. workable	19. _____
20. surmise	e. song-like poem	20. _____
21. cumbersome	f. unleash	21. _____
22. realism	g. outgrowth	22. _____
23. vent	h. refuse	23. _____
24. reject	i. advantage	24. _____
25. practical	j. suppose	25. _____

Dictionary

Pronunciation Guide

Symbol	Example	Symbol	Example
ă	p**a**t	oi	b**oy**
ā	p**ay**	ou	**ou**t
âr	c**are**	o͝o	t**oo**k
ä	f**a**ther	o͞o	b**oo**t
ĕ	p**e**t	ŭ	c**u**t
ē	b**e**	ûr	**ur**ge
ĭ	p**i**t	th	**th**in
ī	p**ie**	*th*	**th**is
îr	p**ier**	hw	**wh**ich
ŏ	p**o**t	zh	vi**s**ion
ō	t**oe**	ə	**a**bout, it**e**m
ô	p**aw**		

Stress Marks: ′(primary); ′(secondary), as in **dictionary** (**dĭk**′shə-nĕr′ē)

A

a·bun·dance (ə **bŭn**′dəns) *n*. An amount that is more than enough; a plentiful or generous supply: *A successful harvest means that there is an abundance of food.*

ac·cu·mu·late (ə **kyo͞om**′yə lāt′) *v.* **ac·cu·mu·lat·ed, ac·cu·mu·lat·ing, ac·cu·mu·lates. 1.** To grow in size or increase gradually: *Ice accumulated in the river over the winter.* **2.** To gather together or collect over time: *The hard-working couple accumulated enough money to retire early.*

ac·quaint·ed (ə **kwānt**′tĭd) *adj.* **1.** Familiar: *I am acquainted with how to use a computer.* **2.** Known to someone else, but not good friends: *Because they are in the same class, they are acquainted.*

a·cute (ə **kyo͞ot**′) *adj.* Less than a 90° angle: *The lines of the triangle were at an acute angle.*

ad·di·tive (**ăd**′ĭ tĭv) *n*. Something added in small amounts to improve quality, change, or preserve something else: *The package label said that there was an additive in the food to make it more nutritious.*

ad·e·quate (**ăd**′ĭ kwĭt) *adj.* As much as is needed; a satisfactory amount; sufficient: *The campers had adequate supplies for the weekend.* —**ad**′**e·quate·ly** *adv.* —**ad**′**e·quate·ness** *n.*

ag·gres·sor (ə **grĕs**′ər) *n*. A person or nation that attacks another without a cause or good reason: *The aggressor in the fight was given an in-school suspension.*

ag·ile (**ăj**′əl *or* **ăj**′īl′) *adj.* Able to move quickly and easily: *The agile gymnast effortlessly performed difficult movements.* —**ag**′**ile·ly** *adv.* —

al·lit·er·a·tion (ə lĭt′ə **rā**′shən) *n*. The repetition of the same beginning letter, sound, or groups of sounds in a series of words: *Tongue twisters often use alliteration.*

am·bas·sa·dor (ăm **băs**′ə dər *or* ăm **băs**′ə dôr′) *n.* **1.** A representative or messenger: *The famous athlete was an ambassador for the shoe company.* **2.** A high government official who represents a country.

am·ple (**ăm**′pəl) *adj.* **am·pler, am·plest. 1.** More than enough: *The amount of food was ample for all the guests.* **2.** Large in size or capacity: *The size of the theater is ample for the school play.* —**am**′**ple·ness** *n.*

a·non·y·mous (ə **nŏn**′ ə məs) *adj.* Unnamed or not identified: *People who use the Internet sometimes want to remain anonymous, so they use a false name.* —**a·non**′**y·mous·ly** *adv.*

an·tique (ăn **tēk**′) *adj.* Belonging to, made in, or in the style of an earlier time: *The antique chair was made during the 1700s.* —*n*. Something made a long time ago: *I bought an antique at the auction.*

ap·pen·dix (ə **pĕn**′dĭks) *n., pl.* **ap·pen·dix·es** or **ap·pen·di·ces** (ə **pĕn**′di sez′). Additional material, tables, or other information at the end of a book: *The appendix of the writing book contained grammar rules.*

ap·pli·ca·tion (ăp′lĭ **kā**′shən) *n.* **1.** A use: *The computer application was successful in solving the problem.* **2.** The act of putting on or into use: *The application of the cream soothed her sunburned skin.* **3.** A request for something such as a job: *I filled out an application for the summer job.*

ap·prox·i·mate (ə **prŏk′** sə mĭt) *adj.* Nearly or almost exact or accurate: *The zoo had a contest to guess the approximate weight of the baby elephant.* —*v.* (ə **prŏk′** sə māt′). **ap·prox·i·mat·ed, ap·prox·i·mat·ing, ap·prox·i·mates.** To come close to or be nearly the same: *The copy of the painting approximates the original.* —**ap·prox′i·mate·ly** *adv.*

ar·chae·ol·o·gy (är′ kē **ŏl′** ə jē) *n.* The scientific study of the life and activities of people who lived in the past: *Archaeologists study the tools, weapons, pottery, buildings, and other things they find.* —**ar′chae·ol′o·gist** *n.*

a·ris·to·crat (ə **rĭs′** tə krăt′ *or* **ăr′** ĭs tə krăt′) *n.* A person of high social position because of birth; nobleman or noblewoman: *The aristocrat attended the queen's dinner.*

as·pect (**ăs′** pĕkt) *n.* **1.** The way something is regarded from a certain viewpoint: *The highway patrol studied the different aspects of the crash to determine its cause.* **2.** The way one or something looks: *Because of his worried aspect, I could tell something was wrong.*

as·sert (ə **sûrt′**) *v.* To state clearly or positively: *The witnesses asserted that they saw one car hit the other.* —**as·sert′er, as·ser′tor** *n.*

as·sort·ment (ə **sôrt′** mənt) *n.* A collection of different kinds; variety: *The candy box contained an assortment of chocolates.*

at·tain (ə **tān′**) *v.* To achieve, accomplish, or gain through work or effort: *The quarterback attained his goal of winning the most games in the league.* —**at·tain′a·bil′i·ty** *n.* —**at·tain′a·ble** *adj.*

au·di·ble (**ô′** də bəl) *adj.* Loud enough to be heard: *My whisper was audible to only those closest to me.* —**au′di·bil′i·ty, au′di·ble·ness** *n.* —**au′di·bly** *adv.*

au·di·tion (ô **dĭsh′** ən) *n.* A trial, hearing, or performance that tests the abilities of a musician, actor, singer, or other performer who is seeking a job: *At the audition for the play, everyone had to read a few lines.* —*v.* To try out for a job in an audition: *All of my friends auditioned for the choir.*

au·di·to·ri·um (ô′ dĭ **tôr′** ē əm) *n., pl.* **au·di·to·ri·ums** or **au·di·to·ri·a. 1.** A large room in a school, church, theater, or other building that is used to seat a large audience: *The band concert was held in the school auditorium.* **2.** A large building used for public gatherings, meetings, or performances.

au·di·to·ry (**ô′** dĭ tôr′ ē) *adj.* Of or relating to hearing, the sense of hearing, or the organs of hearing: *All students had to take an auditory test to check their hearing.*

av·a·lanche (**ăv′** ə lănch′) *n.* **1.** A huge or overwhelming amount: *We receive an avalanche of catalogs in the mail.* **2.** The sudden, fast fall or slide of a great amount of snow, ice, or rocks down a mountain side: *There had been so much snow in the mountains that there was danger of an avalanche.*

B

bal·lad (**băl′** əd) *n.* **1.** A poem that tells a story in simple language and is often intended to be sung: *The class recited and then sang the ballad for their parents.* **2.** A popular love song.

bal·last (**băl′** əst) *n.* Heavy material carried in the lower part of a ship to steady it: *The ship carried ballast because it often sailed through rough seas.*

ban (băn) *v.* **banned, ban·ning, bans.** To forbid officially by law or rule; prohibit: *The city banned the burning of leaves.*

bank·rupt (**băngk′** rŭpt′) *adj.* **1.** Legally declared unable to pay one's debts: *Because nobody shopped at the small store, there wasn't enough money to pay its debts, and the owner was declared bankrupt.* **2.** Completely without money and unable to pay one's debts: *After their expensive vacation the family was bankrupt.* —*n.* A person who is declared unable to pay his or her debts and whose property is divided among the people to whom money is owed. —*v.* To make or cause to become unable to pay one's debts: *Poor money management can bankrupt a person.*

bar·ri·cade (**băr′** ĭ kād′ *or* băr′ ĭ **kād′**) *n.* A structure such as a fence that blocks one's way: *A barricade kept people out of the construction site.* —*v.* **bar·ri·cad·ed, bar·ri·cad·ing, bar·ri·cades.** To block: *The highway patrol barricaded the street.*

be·calmed (bĭ **kämd′**) *adj.* **1.** Made calm or quiet. **2.** Caused to become motionless due to a lack of wind: *The becalmed sailboat waited for the wind to take it out to sea.*

be·friend (bĭ **frĕnd′**) *v.* To act as a friend: *Several students always befriend someone new to the school.*

be·fud·dle (bĭ **fŭd′** l) *v.* To confuse; puzzle: *The unusual play was designed to befuddle our opponents.*

be·moan (bĭ **mōn′**) *v.* To mourn over; grieve for: *Mark Antony's speech bemoaned the cruel death of Caesar.*

bloat·ed (**blō′** tĭd) *adj.* Swollen beyond normal size: *After drinking 10 glasses of water, I felt bloated.*

book·let (**book′** lĭt) *n.* A small book: *The booklet had short articles about each member of the professional basketball team.*

boun·te·ous (**boun′** tē əs) *adj.* **1.** Plentiful; abundant: *The Pilgrims had a bounteous feast the first Thanksgiving.* **2.** Generous: *A bounteous donation was given to the college.* —**boun′te·ous·ly** *adv.* —**boun′te·ous·ness** *n.*

bow (bou) *n.* The front part of a boat or ship: *The bow of the ship had a decoration on it.*

brake (brāk) *n.* A device for slowing or stopping a vehicle or machine: *The brakes on my bicycle are wearing out.* —*v.* To slow or stop with a brake: *A careful driver knows when to brake safely.*

break (brāk) *n.* **1.** A crack or fracture: *Water flowed through the break in the pipe.* **2.** A sudden run: *The dog made a break for the open door.* —*v.* **broke, bro·ken, breaking: 1.** To split or separate into pieces: *I do not want to break my mother's beautiful dishes.* **2.** To fracture: *The hockey player broke his nose.* **3.** To ruin: *I broke the computer.*

bro·cade (brō kād') *n.* A heavy cloth woven with a raised design: *The wedding dress made of brocade was very beautiful and very expensive. v.* **bro·cad·ed, bro·cad·ing, bro·cades.** To weave cloth with a raised design.

bron·co (brŏng' kō) *n., pl.* **bron·cos.** A small wild or partly wild horse or pony found in the western United States: *The bronco was difficult to ride.*

bus·tle (bŭs' əl) *v.* **bus·tled, bus·tling, bus·tles.** To move in a busy, excited, or noisy manner: *Shana bustles around the kitchen when she cooks a meal.* —*n.* Busy, excited, or noisy activity: *The bustle of the playground lasted all day.*

C

ca·ban·a (kə băn' ə *or* kə băn' yə) *n.* A small shelter at a beach or swimming area, used as a bathhouse: *The colorful cabanas provided shelter for the swimmers at the beach.*

cal·ci·um (kăl' sē əm) *n.* A metallic element found in milk and some foods that is essential for the normal growth of bones, teeth, blood, and muscles: *Both children and adults should eat foods rich in calcium to strengthen their bones.*

cal·o·rie (kăl' ə rē) *n.* A unit for measuring energy produced by food: *In order to eat a healthy diet, people should be aware of the number of calories in their food.*

ca·nal (kə năl') *n.* A waterway that is built across land for transportation, irrigation, or drainage: *The Panama Canal greatly shortened the distance a ship had to travel from New York to California.*

ca·pac·i·ty (kə păs' ĭ tē) *n., pl.* **ca·pac·i·ties. 1.** The ability to do something: *The singer had the capacity to sing 1,000 songs from memory.* **2.** The ability to contain, hold, or receive: *The new stadium has a large capacity.* **3.** The maximum amount that can be contained: *The theater has a seating capacity of 400 people.*

cape (kāp) *n.* A point of land jutting out into a large body of water: *People living on a cape enjoy the sea breezes.*

cap·size (kăp' sīz' *or* kăp sīz') *v.* **cap·sized, cap·siz·ing, cap·siz·es.** To overturn: *Everyone got off the boat before it capsized.*

car·go (kär' gō) *n., pl.* **car·goes** *or* **car·gos.** The load of goods or freight carried by a ship, airplane, train, or other vehicle: *When the ship sank, all of its cargo was lost.*

cas·se·role (kăs' ə rōl') *n.* **1.** Food that is both baked and served in the same dish: *The hamburger and potato casserole took an hour to bake.* **2.** A cooking dish in which food is both baked and served: *The glass casserole was too hot to handle.*

cat·a·pult (kăt' ə pŭlt' *or* kăt' ə pŏolt') *v.* **1.** To hurl or shoot forth: *The slingshot catapulted the rock at the target.* **2.** To move suddenly; leap; spring: *We catapulted from our beds when the loud alarm sounded.*

ce·les·tial (sə lĕs' chəl) *adj.* Of or relating to the sky, space, or heavens: *The planets are celestial bodies.* —**ce·les' tial·ly** *adv.*

cho·les·ter·ol (kə lĕs' tə rôl') *n.* A fatty substance contained in many animal and plant tissues that is needed for digestion of fats and production of some hormones. It is thought that large amounts of this substance in the blood may increase the possibility of heart disease. *Mr. Janski was concerned about his cholesterol level.*

cir·cu·late (sûr' kyə lāt') *v.* **cir·cu·lat·ed, cir·cu·lat·ing, cir·cu·lates. 1.** To distribute: *The student council officers circulated a petition asking for a longer lunch period.* **2.** To move freely: *I circulated among the guests at the party.*

cir·cum·fer·ence (sər kŭm' fər əns) *n.* **1.** The outer boundary of a circle: *The dog ran around the circumference of its yard.* **2.** The distance around such a boundary: *The circumference of the track is a mile.*

civ·i·li·za·tion (sĭv' ə lĭ zā' shən) *n.* **1.** The way of life, culture, and society of a particular people, place, and time: *The ancient Egyptian civilization lasted a long time.* **2.** An advanced level of human society in art, science, politics, and social development: *Civilization depends on education.*

clan (klăn) *n.* **1.** A group of families descended from the same ancestor: *The Mays clan attended the funeral of its oldest member.* **2.** A group of people having common interests or background.

cli·mate (klī' mĭt) *n.* **1.** The weather conditions typical of a certain area: *Many people move to Arizona because they like the climate.* **2.** An area having certain weather conditions: *a tropical climate.*

coarse (kôrs) *adj.* **coars·er, coars·est. 1.** Rough; not smooth: *The coarse fabric irritated my skin.* **2.** Made of large particles: *The sand on the beach is coarse.* —**coarse' ly** *adv* —**coarse' ness** *n.*

col·lage (kə **lăzh′**) *n.* Artwork made by pasting or gluing materials such as paper, cloth, metal, string, or other objects onto a surface: *The class made a collage out of dried flowers, seeds, and pictures to show the wildflowers found in their state.*

com·mit·ment (kə **mĭt′** mənt) *n.* **1.** A pledge or obligation: *I made a commitment to volunteer two hours a week at the library.* **2.** The state of being mentally or emotionally tied to another person, thing, or course of action: *A family often shows its commitment to each other during a crisis.*

com·mo·tion (kə **mō′** shən) *n.* Disturbance; disorder: *There was no commotion during the fire because everyone knew what to do.*

com·pre·hend (kŏm′ prĭ **hĕnd′**) *v.* To understand: *I needed several explanations in order to comprehend what had happened.*

con·coct (kən **kŏkt′**) *v.* **1.** To make up; put together; invent: *The team concocted a plan to win the board game.* **2.** To prepare or make by mixing or combining ingredients: *My mother concocted a soup of broth and fresh vegetables.*

con·gru·ent (kŏng′ grōō ənt *or* kən **grōō′** ənt) *adj.* Matching exactly in shape and size: *The rings are congruent.* —**con′ gru·ent·ly** *adv.*

con·sid·er·a·ble (kən **sĭd′** ər ə bəl) *adj.* **1.** Sizable; large: *The amount of garbage a city produces is considerable.* **2.** Important: *The issue of conserving natural resources is considerable.*
—**con·sid′er·a·bly** *adv.*

con·sis·tent (kən **sĭs′** tənt) *adj.* Continually keeping to the same way of acting or thinking: *The children were consistent in doing their homework at the same time every day.* —**con·sis′tent·ly** *adv.*

con·sume (kən **sōōm′**) *v.* **con·sumed, con·sum·ing, con·sumes. 1.** To eat: *The hungry children consumed the entire pizza.* **2.** To use up: *The project consumed all of my free time.*
—**con·sum′a·ble** *adj.*

con·sump·tion (kən **sŭmp′** shən) *n.* **1.** The act of eating: *Consumption of food is necessary for animals to live.* **2.** The amount eaten or used up: *The doctor recommended that I reduce my consumption of chocolate.*

con·ten·tion (kən **tĕn′** shən) *n.* **1.** Disagreement; argument: *The contention was about who was first in line.* **2.** A point argued for: *My parents did not accept my contention that I was too busy to clean my room.*

con·ti·nent (kŏn′ tə nənt) *n.* One of the seven great land areas on the earth. The seven continents are Africa, Antarctica, Asia, Australia, Europe, North America, and South America.

con·trar·y (kŏn′ trĕr ē) *adj.* Opposed; completely different: *The point I made in the discussion was contrary to everyone else's statements.*
—**con′ trar′ i·ly** *adv.* —**con′ trar′ i·ness** *n.*

con·vince (kən **vĭns′**) *v.* **con·vinced, con·vinc·ing, con·vinc·es.** To persuade by argument or with evidence: *My friend convinced me to go to the library to study.*

cor·ral (kə **răl′**) *n.* A fenced-in area for keeping cattle, horses, and other livestock; pen: *The cowboy herded the cattle into the corral for branding.* —*v.* **cor·ralled, cor·ral·ling, cor·rals. 1.** To drive into or hold in a fenced-in area or pen: *The farmer corralled the sheep for shearing.* **2.** To capture or surround: *It was difficult to corral all 12 puppies at once.*

cor·re·spond (kôr′ ĭ **spŏnd′** *or* kŏr′ ĭ **spŏnd′**) *v.* **1.** To communicate by letter: *The pen pals correspond regularly.* **2.** To be in agreement with something: *Snow and ice correspond with the cold weather of winter.*

cor·rupt (kə **rŭpt′**) *adj.* **1.** Dishonest; influenced by bribery; crooked: *The corrupt senator lost the election when the details of her dishonesty were revealed to the voters.* **2.** Wicked; immoral; evil: *The villain in the book lived a corrupt life.* —*v.* To cause to act wickedly or dishonestly: *The dishonest employer tried to corrupt the people who worked for the company.* —**cor·rupt′er** *n.*
—**cor·rupt′ly** *adv.* —**cor·rupt′ness** *n.*

coun·cil (koun′ səl) *n.* **1.** A group of people called together for decision making, discussion, advice, etc.: *The neighbors and I formed a council to discuss the Fourth of July picnic.* **2.** A body of persons elected or appointed to govern or make laws, policies, or decisions: *The city council decided to build a new baseball field.*

coun·sel (koun′ səl) *n.* **1.** Advice: *The counsel my friend gave me was good.* **2.** The exchange of ideas; discussion: *The school board met for counsel on the problem.* —*v.* **coun·seled, coun·sel·ling, coun·sels** *or* **coun·selled, coun·sel·ling.** To give advice; advise: *The teacher counseled the class to study.*

cou·plet (kŭp′ lĭt) *n.* A pair of lines that end with the same sound and have the same beat: *Shakespeare often used couplets in his plays.*

course (kôrs) *n.* **1.** Onward movement from one point to the next: *My spelling improved over the course of the school year.* **2.** The route or direction something moves: *The bus follows the same course every day.* **3.** An area where some races or games are held: *The cross-country track team races on a course that goes through the woods.* **4.** A class: *The speed reading course helped me read faster.*

crafts·man (krăfts′ mən) *n.* A skilled worker: *The craftsman created a beautiful sculpture.*
—**crafts′ man·ship** *n.*

crave (krāv) *v.* **craved, crav·ing, craves.** To want, long for, or desire strongly: *When I go to the movies, I crave popcorn.*

cred·it (krĕd′ĭt) *n.* **1.** A plan that gives permission to pay over a period of time: *Because cars cost so much, many people buy them on credit.* **2.** Trust in one's reputation and ability to meet payments when due: *The store checked to see if I had a good credit rating.*

crim·i·nol·o·gy (krĭm′ə **nŏl**′ə jē) *n.* The scientific study of crime, criminals, and corrections: *Experts in criminology often use observation skills.* —**crim**′**i·nol**′**o·gist** *n.*

cul·ture (kŭl′chər) *n.* The skills, arts, and customs that make up a way of life of a certain people at a certain time: *The class studied the culture of the Chinese.*

cum·ber·some (kŭm′bər səm) *adj.* Difficult to carry or manage; awkward: *The big box was too cumbersome for one person to carry.* —**cum**′**ber·some·ly** *adv.* —**cum**′**ber·some·ness** *n.*

cur·few (kûr′fyo͞o) *n.* A rule or order requiring people to be off the streets and indoors or at home by a certain time: *The curfew on school nights was 10:00.*

cur·ren·cy (kûr′ən sē *or* kŭr′ən sē) *n., pl.* **cur·ren·cies.** The type of money that is in circulation in a country: *Some people collect currency from foreign countries.*

cy·lin·dri·cal (sə **lĭn**′drĭ kəl) *adj.* Having the form of a figure that is bounded by a curved surface and two equal parallel circles at the ends: *The aluminum can has a cylindrical shape.* —**cy·lin**′**dri·cal·ly** *adv.*

D

daunt·ing (dônt′ĭng *or* dänt′ĭng) *adj.* Discouraging; frightening: *Columbus faced the daunting task of sailing across an ocean for which there were no maps.*

daw·dle (dôd′l) *v.* **daw·dled, daw·dling, daw·dles.** To waste time; take more time than necessary: *I missed my bus because I dawdled over breakfast.* —**daw**′**dler** *n.*

de·bris (də **brē**′ *or* dā′brē′) *n.* The remains, bits, and pieces of something broken or destroyed: *After the tornado, debris from buildings was scattered everywhere.*

de·ceive (dĭ **sēv**′) *v.* **de·ceived, de·ceiv·ing, de·ceives.** To make someone believe something that is not true; to trick: *The quotation deceived the listeners because it was taken out of context.* —**de·ceiv**′**er** *n.*

de·cep·tion (dĭ sĕp′shən) *n.* A trick: *When I discovered my friend's deception, I was angry.*

de·ci·pher (dĭ **sī**′fər) *v.* **1.** To interpret or translate from a code to ordinary language; decode: *The expert was able to decipher the enemy's code.* **2.** To make out the meaning of something hard to read or understand: *The teacher tried to decipher the student's handwriting.* —**de·ci**′**pher·a·ble** *adj.*

de·fi·cien·cy (dĭ **fĭsh**′ən sē) *n., pl.* **de·fi·cien·cies.** Shortage; a lack of something necessary: *I had to drink more milk because I had a deficiency of calcium in my diet.*

de·jec·tion (dĭ **jĕk**′shən) *n.* Sadness; low spirits: *When my best friend moved away, my dejection lasted until I visited her.*

de·pend·a·ble (dĭ **pĕn**′də bəl) *adj.* Reliable; trustworthy: *Since my sister is dependable, I can always count on her.* —**de·pend**′**a·bil**′**i·ty** *n.* —**de·pend**′**a·bly** *adv.*

de·pend·ent (dĭ **pĕn**′dənt) *adj.* Relying on or influenced by on another person or something else: *The location of the picnic is dependent on the weather.* —**de·pend**′**ent·ly** *adv.*

de·pres·sion (dĭ **prĕsh**′ən) *n.* **1.** An area that has sunk below its surroundings; hollow: *The depression in the land was caused by an underground spring.* **2.** Sadness: *The girl's depression lasted for a few hours.*

de·ri·sive (dĭ **rī**′sĭv *or* dĭ **rī**′zĭv) *adj.* Mocking, ridiculing, or making fun of something: *Critics made derisive remarks about the bad dialogue in the movie.* —**de·ri**′**sive·ly** *adv.* —**de·ri**′**sive·ness** *n.*

de·vise (dĭ **vīz**′) *v.* **de·vised, de·vis·ing, de·vis·es.** To form, create, or work out: *The class devised a plan for its room decorations.* —**de·vis**′**er** *n.*

dil·i·gent (dĭl′ə jənt) *adj.* Determined, careful, and hard-working: *With diligent research, scientists discovered a cure for the disease.*

dis·charge (dĭs′chärj′ *or* dĭs **chärj**′) *n.* A sudden release or letting out: *The government should regulate the discharge of pollutants into the air.* —*v.* **dis·charged, dis·charg·ing, dis·charg·es.** To release or let out: *A sneeze discharges germs into the air.*

dis·miss (dĭs **mĭs**′) *v.* **1.** To order or allow to leave: *The judge will dismiss the jury after the trial.* **2.** To put out of one's thoughts: *The chairperson dismissed our suggestion before we could explain it.*

dis·pute (dĭ **spyo͞ot**′) *v.* **dis·put·ed, dis·put·ing, dis·putes.** To argue over or about; debate: *The city council members disputed whether or not to raise taxes.*

dis·rupt (dĭs **rŭpt**′) *v.* To throw into disorder or confusion; disturb or interrupt: *The loud shouting in the hallway disrupted the class.* —**dis·rupt**′**er** *n.*

dom·i·nant (dŏm′ə nənt) *adj.* Having the most influence, power, or control; most important: *The dominant stallion in a herd of wild horses protects the other horses.* —**dom**′**i·nant·ly** *adv.*

dy·nas·ty (dī′nə stē) *n., pl.* **dy·nas·ties.** A series of rulers from the same family: *The history book explained the Egyptian dynasties.*

E

ec·o·nom·i·cal (ĕk′ə **nŏm′**ĭ kəl *or* ē′kə **nŏm′**ĭ kəl) *adj.* Not wasting money or goods; careful in using money: *The economical woman compared prices before she bought anything.*

e·ject (ĭ **jĕkt′**) *v.* To throw out or force out: *The people who talked loudly during the movie were ejected.*

em·a·nate (ĕm′ə nāt′) *v.* **em·a·nat·ed, em·a·nat·ing, em·a·nates.** To send forth; to come forth: *The pleasant odor of baking bread emanated from the kitchen.*

em·per·or (ĕm′pər ər) *n.* The male ruler of an empire: *The emperor announced a new law.*

en·coun·ter (ĕn **koun′**tər) *v.* To meet or come upon unexpectedly: *I did not expect to encounter my friend at the mall.* —*n.* An unexpected meeting: *The encounter of the friends was a pleasant surprise.*

en·croach (ĕn **krōch′**) *v.* **en·croached, en·croach·ing, en·croach·es. 1.** To go beyond proper, natural, or normal limits: *During the flood the river encroached on the fields.* **2.** To take over or trepass on the rights or property of another: *Conservationists said that the housing development would encroach on the natural feeding grounds of the deer.*

en·dear (ĕn **dîr′**) *v.* To make dearly loved: *The woman's kindness endeared her to everyone who knew her.* —**en·dear′ing·ly** *adv.*

en·er·get·ic (ĕn′ər **jĕt′**ĭk) *adj.* Having, showing, or using great energy; powerful; forceful: *The coach was so energetic that he inspired the team to do well.*

en·gulf (ĕn **gŭlf′**) *v.* To swallow up; overwhelm: *The sea engulfed the* Titanic *in just a few hours.*

en·tic·ing (ĕn **tīs′**ĭng) *adj.* Tempting or attractive: *The smell of the turkey was enticing.*

en·voy (ĕn′voi′ *or* ŏn′voi′) *n.* **1.** A government representative who is sent by one country to another: *The envoy took the president's message to the king of the other country.* **2.** A messenger or representative.

e·rup·tion (ĭ **rŭp′**shən) *n.* The act of throwing forth something suddenly and violently: *The eruption of fire, smoke, and lava from Mt. Vesuvius destroyed the Italian city of Pompeii.*

es·ca·pade (ĕs′kə pād′) *n.* A reckless adventure, undertaking, or prank: *The hero's escapades kept our attention throughout the entire movie.*

es·teem (ĭ **stēm′**) *n.* Favorable regard; respect: *Our principal is held in high esteem by both students and parents.* —*v.* To regard with respect; value: *The senator is esteemed for her sincerity and honesty.*

ev·i·dent (ĕv′ĭ dənt) *adj.* Easy to see or understand; clear: *The comet was evident in the sky on clear nights.*

e·voke (ĭ **vōk′**) *v.* **e·voked, e·vok·ing, e·vokes. 1.** To call to mind; stir up: *The music evoked memories of the school musical production.* **2.** To bring forth: *The rude question evoked an angry answer from the teacher.*

ex·ag·ger·a·tion (ĭg zăj′ə **rā′**shən) *n.* A statement that makes the truth greater or larger than it really is; overstatement: *Everybody knew that the child's story was an exaggeration of what really happened.*

ex·cerpt (ĕk′sûrpt′) *n.* A passage or selection taken from a larger work, such as a book or play: *The speaker quoted an excerpt from a novel that related to the topic.* —*v.* To select or take out a passage or selection: *The assignment was to excerpt and explain passages from famous speeches.*

ex·clude (ĭk **sklo͞od′**) *v.* **excluded, excluding, excludes.** To keep from entering: *The rules of the park exclude children unless they are accompanied by a parent.*

ex·clu·sive (ĭk **sklo͞o′**sĭv) *adj.* **1.** Leaving out some who are not part of a select group: *The principal gave an exclusive interview to the beginning student reporter.* **2.** Not divided or shared with others: *The singer has exclusive rights to profits from the new CD.* **3.** Entire: *During the timeout the coach had the exclusive attention of the players.* —**ex·clu′sive·ly** *adv.* —**ex·clu′sive·ness** *n.*

ex·cur·sion (ĭk **skûr′**zhən) *n.* **1.** A usually short trip made for a special purpose or for pleasure: *We took an excursion to the river bluffs to see the bald eagles.* **2.** A round trip on a plane, bus, train, ship, or other passenger vehicle at a reduced rate: *The travel agency arranged an affordable weekend excursion to the football game.*

ex·pen·di·ture (ĭk **spĕn′**də chər) *n.* **1.** The act of spending or paying out: *Congress discussed an expenditure for public transportation.* **2.** Something that is spent or paid out, such as money or time: *Homework requires a great expenditure of my time.*

ex·ploits (ĕk′sploits′) *n.* Daring or heroic acts or deeds: *The many exploits of firefighters make them heroes.*

ex·tra·cur·ric·u·lar (ĕk′strə kə **rĭk′**yə lər) *adj.* Not part of the regular course of study of a school: *The French Club is an extracurricular activity that helps students learn about France.*

ex·tra·dite (ĕk′strə dīt′) *v.* **ex·tra·dit·ed, ex·tra·dit·ing, ex·tra·dites.** To turn over, deliver, or surrender (a person accused of a crime) for trial to the authorities of a city, state, or country where the crime was committed: *The accused bank robber was extradited from Florida to New York for trial.*

ex·tra·ne·ous (ĭk **strā′**nē əs) *n.* **1.** Not related to the subject; not essential; irrelevant: *The story about getting lost on the way to the movie is extraneous* to information about whether the movie is good or not. **2.** Coming from the outside; foreign: *The glass of water had extraneous matter in it.* —**ex·tra′ne·ous·ly** *adv.* —**ex·tra′ne·ous·ness** *n.*

ex·tra·sen·so·ry (ĕk′strə sĕn′sə rē) *adj.* Outside of, beyond, or apart from the normal range or perception of the senses: *Some people seem to have an extrasensory ability to predict weather changes.*

ex·trav·a·gant (ĭk străv′ə gənt) *adj.* **1.** Spending money unwisely or wastefully: *When the bills arrived, I regretted my extravagant shopping trip.* **2.** Costing too much; more than is reasonable: *The price of the name brand skates seemed extravagant, so I bought a more reasonably priced pair.* —**ex·trav′a·gant·ly** *adv.*

ex·trude (ĭk strōōd′) *v.* **ex·trud·ed, ex·trud·ing, ex·trudes. 1.** To push or force out: *Squeezing the tube, extrudes toothpaste.* **2.** To stick out: *The gel extruded from the broken container.*

ex·ul·ta·tion (ĕk′səl tā′shən *or* ĕg′zəl tā′shən) *n.* Great rejoicing; great happiness and celebration: *Everyone who helped make the movie felt a sense of exultation at the grand opening.*

F

fac·et (făs′ĭt) *n.* A phase, side, or aspect: *People's busy lives have many different facets.*

fam·ine (făm′ĭn) *n.* A very great and widespread shortage of food: *The country's famine was due to a change in climate that made it impossible to grow food.*

fi·ber (fī′bər) *n.* The part of grains, fruits, and vegetables that cannot be digested and absorbed by the body: *I eat bran cereal every day to add fiber to my diet.*

fig·ment (fĭg′mənt) *n.* Something made up or imagined: *Even though the events in the book seemed real, they were figments of the author's imagination.*

fi·nan·cial (fə năn′shəl *or* fī năn′shəl) *adj.* Having to do with money matters or managing money: *The bank had a meeting to discuss its financial future.* —**fi·nan′cial·ly** *adv.*

for·bear·ance (fôr bâr′əns) *n.* Patience, tolerance, self-control: *The candidate showed forbearance when answering the difficult questions.*

fore·tell (fôr tĕl′) *v.* **fore·told, fore·tell·ing, fore·tells.** To tell beforehand; predict: *Some people claim that they have the ability to foretell the future.*

for·mal·ly (fôr′məl lē) *adv.* **1.** Officially: *The president of the company formally announced his resignation.* **2.** Properly: *I was formally introduced to the governor.*

for·mer·ly (fôr′mər lē) *adv.* In times past; previously: *The news anchor formerly worked for a competing television station.*

frac·ture (frăk′chər) *n.* A breaking or break, split, or crack, as in a bone: *The football player had to wear a cast while the fracture of the bone in his arm healed.* —*v.* **frac·tured, frac·tur·ing, frac·tures.** To break, split, or crack or cause to break, split, or crack: *I fractured my wrist when I fell.*

frag·ile (frăj′əl *or* frăj′īl′) *adj.* Easily broken or damaged; delicate: *The fragile dishes are kept where the toddler cannot reach them.*

frag·ment (frăg′mənt) *n.* **1.** A small part or piece that is broken off: *We found fragments of the broken cup under the table.* **2.** An incomplete or unfinished part: *The sound system was so bad that we could hear only fragments of the speech.* —*v.* To break into small parts or pieces: *The icicle fragmented when it fell off the house.*

frail (frāl) *adj.* **1.** Physically weak; not strong: *The sick old woman was very frail.* **2.** Easily torn or broken: *The pages in the antique book were frail.* **3.** Easily tempted; weak in character: *Evil people may take advantage of others who have frail characters.* —**frail′ness** *n.*

fru·gal (frōō′gəl) *adj.* **1.** Careful in spending money; not wasteful: *Rather than throw away the stale bread, the frugal cook used it to make stuffing.* **2.** Inexpensive; of little amount: *The poor family had a frugal meal.* —**fru·gal′i·ty** *n.* **fru′gal·ly** *adv.*

G

ge·ol·o·gy (jē ŏl′ə jē) *n., pl.* **ge·ol·o·gies. 1.** The science that deals with the earth's origin, history, structure, rocks, and fossils: *In geology class I learned to identify different kinds of rocks.* **2.** The structure and composition of the earth in a specific region. *The geology of the Grand Canyon reveals much about the history of the earth.* —**ge·ol′o·gist** *n.*

gla·cier (glā′shər) *n.* A large mass of slowly moving ice: *Early glaciers created many valleys and hills in parts of North America.*

gorge (gôrj) *v.* **gorged, gorg·ing, gorg·es. 1.** To stuff with food: *We gorged ourselves on popcorn, cotton candy, and ice cream at the fair.* **2.** To eat greedily: *When he finally ate, the starving man was so hungry that he gorged his food.*

grat·i·fy (grăt′ə fī′) *v.* **grat·i·fied, grat·i·fy·ing, grat·i·fies.** To satisfy or please: *I was gratified by the news that my favorite charity reached its goal.* —*adj.* **grat·i·fy·ing.** Satisfying: *Helping others in need is gratifying.*

H

hab·i·tat (hăb′ĭ tăt′) *n.* **1.** The place or region where a plant or animal naturally lives: *When the natural habitat of an animal is destroyed, it may become endangered.* **2.** The place where a person is usually found. *The library is Leroy's usual habitat.*

heed (hēd) *v.* To pay attention to: *I fell on the ice when I did not heed the warning that the walks were slippery.* —*n.* Close attention: *The students paid no heed to the teacher's request to stop talking.*

hem·i·sphere (hĕm′ĭ sfîr′) *n.* One-half of the earth's surface. The equator divides the earth into the northern and southern hemispheres and the Greenwich meridian divides the earth into the eastern and western hemispheres. *Canada is in the northern hemisphere.*

her·ald (hĕr′əld) *v.* To announce or be a sign of: *Advertisements for back-to-school clothes herald the start of a new school year.* —*n.* A person or thing that is a sign of something to come: *A smile indicated that my friend was a herald of good news.*

hi·er·o·glyph·ic (hī′ər ə glĭf′ĭk *or* hī′rə glĭf′ĭk) *adj.* Of, relating to, or made up of pictures or symbols that represent words, syllables, sounds, or objects: *The hieroglyphic writings of the Egyptians help people understand their ancient civilization.* —**hi′er·o·glyph′i·cal·ly** *adv.*

I

im·age·ry (ĭm′ĭj rē) *n., pl.* **im·age·ries.** The use of words and language to create vivid descriptions: *I was able to see the picture in my mind because of the imagery used in the poem.*

im·pact (ĭm′păkt′) *n.* **1.** The force of one thing hitting another; collision: *The impact of the two cars caused much damage.* **2.** An effect or influence: *The favorable impact of the new safety rules was noticed immediately.*

im·pose (ĭm pōz′) *v.* **im·posed, im·pos·ing, im·pos·es. 1.** To place, establish, or apply by authority: *The government imposed a larger tax on personal income.* **2.** To force: *Steve imposed his ideas on his friends.*

in·au·gu·rate (ĭn ô′gyə rāt′) *v.* **in·au·gu·rat·ed, in·au·gu·rat·ing, in·au·gu·rates. 1.** To begin officially or formally: *The lighting of the official torch inaugurates the Olympic Games.* **2.** To install in office with a formal ceremony: *The president is inaugurated in January.*

in·dus·tri·ous (ĭn dŭs′trē əs) *adj.* Working steadily and tirelessly: *The industrious students produced a prize-winning science project.*

in·fringe (ĭn frĭnj′) *v.* To intrude or invade upon without a right; trespass: *The Supreme Court ruled that the new law was unconstitutional because it infringed on the right of free speech.*

in·ject (ĭn jĕkt′) *v.* **1.** To force or drive (a fluid or gas) into something: *The mechanic injected air into the tires.* **2.** To force (a fluid or medicine) through the skin into a muscle, vein, or other body part: *The doctor injected the vaccine into the muscle in the arm.* —**in·jec′tor** *n.*

in·ter·mis·sion (ĭn tər mĭsh′ən) *n.* The time between periods of activity, such as acts of a play: *We went to the lobby for refreshments during the intermission of the play.*

in·ter·plan·e·tar·y (ĭn tər plăn′ĭ tĕr′ē) *adj.* Between planets: *Many science fiction stories include interplanetary travel.*

in·ter·sect (ĭn′tər sĕct′) *v.* **1.** To divide by cutting across or through: *The railroad tracks intersect the town.* **2.** To cross each other: *The accident happened where the two highways intersect.*

i·so·lat·ed (ī′sə lā′tĭd) *adj.* Separated or set apart from others: *Because everyone else had gone to the movies, I felt isolated at home by myself.*

isth·mus (ĭs′məs) *n., pl.* **isth·mus·es** *or* **isth·mi.** A narrow strip of land having water on both sides and connecting two larger masses of land: *Traveling over an isthmus from one body of water to another may not take very long.*

J

jet·ti·son (jĕt′ĭ sən *or* jĕt′ĭ zən) *v.* To throw or cast something (cargo, equipment, fuel) overboard so as to lighten the load: *The captain jettisoned the ship's cargo when its hull began to leak.*

joc·u·lar (jŏk′yə lər) *adj.* **1.** Liking to joke; playful: *The jocular clown made everyone laugh.* **2.** Meant as a joke; funny: *The teacher made a jocular remark.* —**joc′u·lar′i·ty** *n.* —**joc′u·lar·ly** *adv.*

K

knot (nŏt) *n.* A unit of speed used by boats that equals one nautical mile per hour or approximately 6,076 feet per hour: *The motorboat was traveling at four knots.*

L

lar·i·at (lăr′ē ət) *n.* A long rope with a loop at one end that is used for catching horses and other livestock: *The young cowboy had to practice a long time before he was able to use a lariat to rope a horse.*

leaf·let (lē′flĭt) *n.* A single sheet of printed matter that is often folded; flyer: *To advertise my lawn care business, I gave my neighbors leaflets explaining my services.*

lee·ward (lē′wərd *or* lōō′ərd) *adj.* On or moving toward the direction or side which the wind is blowing: *The palm trees are on the leeward side of the island.* —*n.* The direction or side toward which the wind is blowing.

leg·en·dar·y (lĕj′ən dĕr′ē) *adj.* **1.** Based on a story, that may be based on some facts, that has been told so often that it is thought to be true: *The story of King Arthur and Camelot is legendary.* **2.** Famous: *The award-winning movie director is legendary.*

lev·er·age (lĕv′ər ĭj *or* lē′vər ĭj) *n.* An increased advantage or power to act: *Whoever has the remote control has the leverage to choose a television show.*

lin·e·age (lĭn′ē ĭj) *n.* A line of direct descent from an ancestor: *Priscilla traced her lineage to a signer of the Declaration of Independence.*

lum·ber (lŭm′bər) *v.* To move or walk slowly, clumsily, or noisily: *The overweight dog lumbered down the sidewalk.*

lure (lo͝or) *v.* **lured, lur·ing, lures.** To tempt or attract powerfully: *The food lured the cat out of the tree.* —*n.* Something that tempts or attracts: *The chance to win a prize was the lure used to get people to enter the contest.*

lyr·ic poem (lĭr′ĭk pō′əm) *n.* A type of poetry that expresses strong personal emotions: *The lyric poem expressed the writer's sadness.*

M

make·shift (māk′shĭft′) *adj.* Of, used, or like a substitute: *The elderly person used a broomstick as a makeshift cane.* —*n.* Something used as a substitute: *I didn't have an umbrella, so I used a newspaper as a makeshift.*

mal·ad·just·ed (măl′ə jŭs′tĭd) *adj.* Poorly or badly adjusted to one's surroundings, environment, or circumstances: *The tiger was maladjusted to its life in the zoo.*

mal·con·tent (măl′kən tĕnt′) *adj.* Unhappy or dissatisfied with current conditions: *The workers were malcontent with the long hours they had to work.* —*n.* A person who is unhappy or dissatisfied with current conditions: *Nothing ever satisfies a malcontent.*

mal·formed (măl fôrmd′) *adj.* Having an abnormal, faulty, or imperfect form: *A frog with five legs is malformed.*

mal·func·tion (măl fŭngk′shən) *n.* The failure to function properly: *A malfunction of the car's lights caused an accident.* —*v.* To fail to function or work properly: *A power surge may cause a computer to malfunction.*

mal·nu·tri·tion (măl′no͞o trĭsh′ən *or* măl′nyo͞o trĭsh′ən) *n.* A condition caused by a lack of enough food or food with essential vitamins and minerals: *People were shocked when they saw the pictures of the children suffering from malnutrition.*

mal·prac·tice (măl prăk′tĭs) *n.* **1.** Improper, careless, or harmful treatment of a patient by a doctor: *Even though the patient died, there was no evidence of malpractice by the doctor.* **2.** Improper or wrong conduct by a professional, such as a lawyer, in an official position: *The lawyer lost his license to practice law because of malpractice.*

man·a·cle (măn′ə kəl) *n.* **1.** Handcuffs: *The accused murderer wore manacles to the trial.* **2.** Something that restricts freedom. —*v.* **man·a·cled, man·a·cling, man·a·cles. 1.** To put handcuffs on: *The police manacled the burglar.* **2.** To restrict or restrain: *The time limit manacled our ability to study the problem thoroughly.*

man·age (măn′ĭj) *v.* **man·aged, man·ag·ing, man·ag·es. 1.** To guide, direct, control, or be in charge of: *The best workers were taught how to manage their departments.* **2.** To succeed in doing something: *The busy mother was able to manage both her career and her family.* **3.** To get along: *The class managed to learn even when the teacher was ill.*

man·i·cure (măn′ĭ kyo͝or′) *n.* The cleaning, trimming, and polishing of the fingernails: *The manicure made my fingernails look pretty.*

man·u·al (măn′yo͞o əl) *adj.* **1.** Relating to or involving the hands: *The delicate sewing project required manual skill.* **2.** Operated by the hands: *Pilots have to know how to operate the manual controls of an airplane.* —**man′u·al·ly** *adv.*

man·u·fac·ture (măn′yə făk′chər) *v.* **man·u·fac·tured, man·u·fac·tur·ing, man·u·fac·tures. 1.** To make or produce a product, especially a large amount, by using machines: *The factory manufactures parts for shoes.* **2.** To make up: *The children manufactured an excuse for their tardiness.* —*n.* The act or process of making or producing a product: *The manufacture of toys is a big industry.*

meg·a·byte (mĕg′ə bīt′) *n.* A computer term that means one million bytes. One byte can store a single alphabetical or numerical character or symbol: *Before I bought a new computer, I researched the number of megabytes I needed.*

meg·a·lith (mĕg′ə lĭth′) *n.* A huge stone used in prehistoric monuments: *People can only guess how the prehistoric people were able to move the megaliths used in their monuments.*

meg·a·phone (mĕg′ə fōn′) *n.* A cone-shaped horn used to increase the volume of the voice: *The principal used a megaphone to direct students during the fire drill.*

me·ter (mē′tər) *n.* The pattern of accented and unaccented syllables in a line of poetry; pattern of stress or beats: *The meter of the poem was so clear that we tapped our toes as we read.*

mi·cro·or·gan·ism (mī′krō ôr′gə nĭz′əm) *n*. An organism such as a bacterium that can only be seen through a microscope: *The science class studied microorganisms found in ponds.*

mi·cro·wave (mī′krō wāv′) *n*. A high-frequency electromagnetic wave with a wavelength from one millimeter to one meter. It is used in radar, for long-distance transmission of television signals, and in cooking: *A microwave oven can heat food in just a minute or two.*

mi·grate (mī′grāt′) *v*. **mi·grat·ed, mi·grat·ing, mi·grates. 1.** To move from one place, region, or country to another: *The pioneers migrated to the West.* **2.** To move to another region with the change of seasons: *Monarch butterflies migrate to Mexico for the winter.*

mi·ser (mī′z/r) *n*. A person who saves money for the sake of saving it and rarely spends it: *Because the miser rarely spent money, nobody knew that he was wealthy.*

mis·sion·ar·y (mĭsh′ə nĕr′ē) *n., pl.* **mis·sion·ar·ies.** A person who is sent, usually by a religious organization, to spread its religion or do charitable work, especially in a foreign country: *The missionary converted many people to his religion.*

mo·ti·vate (mō′tə vāt′) *v*. **mo·ti·vat·ed, mo·ti·vat·ing, mo·ti·vates.** To move to action: *The music teacher tried to motivate her piano students to practice more.*

N

nar·ra·tive (năr′ə tĭv) *n*. A type of story or account: *The audience listened to the narrative about the expedition to the South Pole.*

neb·u·lous (nĕb′yə ləs) *adj*. Vague; unclear: *The teacher's nebulous answer only confused the class.* —**neb′u·lous·ly** *adv*. —**neb′u·lous·ness** *n*.

neg·li·gent (nĕg′lĭ jənt) *adj*. Not showing or doing what should be done properly; careless; thoughtless: *The negligent driver did not stop for the red light and almost caused an accident.* —**neg′li·gent·ly** *adv*.

neg·li·gi·ble (nĕg′lĭ jə bəl) *adj*. Not worth considering: *The amount of snow was negligible, so I didn't have to shovel the walks.* —**neg′li·gi·bly** *adv*.

ne·go·ti·ate (nĭ gō′shē āt′) *v*. **ne·go·ti·at·ed, ne·go·ti·at·ing, ne·go·ti·ates. 1.** To succeed in going over, crossing, passing over, or coping with: *The mountain climber was able to negotiate the the steep cliff.* **2.** To discuss, bring about, settle, or arrange: *The lawyers negotiated a settlement of the lawsuit.* —**ne·go′ti·a′tor** *n*.

nim·ble (nĭm′bəl) *adj*. **nim·bler, nim·blest. 1.** Quick and light in movement: *The nimble dancer seemed to fly across the stage.* **2.** Quick to understand or think: *The nimble contestant knew the answers to the questions before anyone else.* —**nim′ble·ness** *n*. —**nim′bly** *adv*.

no·bil·i·ty (nō bĭl′ĭ tē) *n., pl.* **no·bil·i·ties.** A class of people having high birth, rank, and often wealth, power, and privilege: *The nobility lost their privileges during the French Revolution.*

nov·el·ette (nŏv′ə lĕt′) *n*. A short novel: *I was able to read the entire novelette during the airplane flight.*

O

ob·jec·tion (əb jĕk′shən) *n*. **1.** A reason for disapproving or disliking: *My objection to the toy drum was that it made too much noise.* **2.** A statement of disapproval or opposition: *Many parents voiced their objections concerning the new class schedule to the school board.*

ob·tuse (əb tōōs′ *or* əb tyōōs′) *adj*. Greater than a 90-degree angle but less than a 180-degree angle: *The obtuse angle measures 120 degrees.*

on·set (ŏn′sĕt′ *or* ôn′sĕt′) *n*. A beginning; start: *Snowflakes and a strong wind marked the onset of the blizzard.*

op·e·ret·ta (ŏp′ə rĕt′ə) *n*. A short musical play that is similar to an opera but is light and amusing and contains music and song that are combined with spoken dialogue: *The audience thoroughly enjoyed the operetta performed by the students.*

or·gan·ic (ôr găn′ĭk) *adj*. Produced or grown by methods that do not use chemical fertilizers, insecticides, or other artificial substances: *The vegetable market sold only vegetables that were grown using organic methods.* —**or·gan′i·cal·ly** *adv*.

o·ver·whelm·ing (ō′vər wĕl′ming) *adj*. Too great in effect or strength to be overcome; overpowering: *At first the difficult history project seemed overwhelming.*

P

par·al·lel (păr′ə lĕl′) *adj*. Going in the same direction and being the same distance apart from each other so as to never meet: *The tracks on a roller coaster are parallel.*

parched (pärcht) *adj*. Very dry, especially from heat: *The strong wind blew the parched desert sand into the nomads' tents.*

pass·port (păs′pôrt′) *n*. **1.** Something that gives or assures a person of success or acceptance: *Practice is a musician's passport to success.* **2.** A document issued by a government to a citizen that identifies the person and allows him or her to travel to other countries: *You need a passport to travel from the United States to France.*

peas·ant (pĕz′ ənt) *n.* A member of a class of small farmers and farm laborers: *The peasants worked very hard but were not able to make much money.*

pen·du·lum (pĕn′ jə ləm *or* pĕn′ dyə ləm) *n.* An object hung from a fixed point that swings back and forth to regulate something like a clock: *The clock's pendulum stopped when I bumped the clock.*

pen·in·su·la (pə nĭn′ syə lə *or* pə nĭn′ sə lə) *n.* A land mass almost entirely surrounded by water and projecting out from a larger land mass: *The peninsula of Florida has the Atlantic Ocean on the east and the Gulf of Mexico on the west.*

pen·sion (pĕn′ shən) *n.* A payment of money, not wages, paid to a retired or disabled person: *The elderly man's pension was enough for him to live comfortably.*

per·ceive (pər sēv′) *v.* **per·ceived, per·ceiv·ing, per·ceives.** To become aware of something through the five senses: *As we approached the restaurant, we perceived the smell of cooking food.* **—per·ceiv′er** *n.*

per·cep·tion (pər sĕp′ shən) *n.* An understanding or observation: *My perception of the facts was different from my brother's.*

per·pen·dic·u·lar (pûr′ pən dĭk′ yə lər) *adj.* At right angles to a line or surface: *The goal post is perpendicular to the field.*

per·son·al (pûr′ sə nəl) *adj.* **1.** Concerning or relating to a particular person and his or her private life; individual: *The personal letter from the college student expressed feelings of loneliness.* **2.** Done or made in person: *The actor made a personal appearance at the party.*

per·son·nel (pûr sə nĕl′) *n.* Persons working in a company, organization, or other place of business: *The company's personnel were happy with their pay increases.*

pes·ti·cide (pĕs′ tĭ sīd′) *n.* A chemical used to kill harmful insects, plants, or animals: *A pesticide was used to kill the rats.*

phys·i·ol·o·gy (fĭz′ ē ŏl′ ə jē) *n.* The science that deals with the functions and activities of living things and their parts: *Students who want to be doctors must take physiology classes.* **—phys′ i·ol′ o·gist** *n.*

plat·i·num (plăt′ n əm) *n.* An expensive heavy silver-white metal that is resistant to corrosion and is used in industrial equipment, jewelry, and dentistry: *As the use of platinum in jewelry increased, so did its price.*

pon·der (pŏn′ dər) *v.* To think about thoroughly and carefully: *In order to solve the crime, the detective had to ponder all the evidence.*

por·ter (pôr′ tər) *n.* **1.** A person who carries luggage for others, as in a hotel: *The porter carried the hotel guest's suitcases to her room.* **2.** An attendant who helps or waits on passengers in a railway car.

por·tray (pôr trā′) *v.* **1.** To describe in words: *The biography portrayed Martin Luther King as a heroic man.* **2.** To show in a picture: *The artist portrayed the queen in an oil painting.* **3.** To play the part of on stage, in a movie, or on television: *The actress portrayed Eleanor Roosevelt in the movie.*

pov·er·ty (pŏv′ ər tē) *n.* The state of being poor: *The money from the charity was used to help relieve the poverty of the people.*

prac·ti·cal (prăk′ tĭ kəl) *adj.* **1.** Capable of working, being done, carried out, or used; workable: *Because I finished my homework quickly, I know that my plan for doing it is practical.* **2.** Coming from use, action, or experience rather than study or thought: *Taking care of my little brother and sister has given me practical experience in babysitting.* **—prac′ ti·cal′ i·ty** *n.*

prai·rie (prâr′ ē) *n.* A large area of flat or nearly flat grassland and few trees: *The prairies of the Midwest are excellent for farming.*

pre·car·i·ous (prĭ kâr′ ē əs) *adj.* **1.** Dangerous: *When the rope broke, the mountain climber was in a precarious position.* **2.** Dependent upon chance; uncertain: *Without wise planning, our future is precarious.* **—pre·car′ i·ous·ly** *adv.*

pre·ser·va·tive (prĭ zûr′ və tĭv) *n.* Something used or added to foods to keep or slow them from spoiling: *A preservative was added to the bacon so that it would not spoil so quickly.*

pre·sume (prĭ zōōm′) *v.* **pre·sumed, pre·sum·ing, pre·sumes.** To believe to be true; take for granted; suppose: *The driver of the school bus presumed that everyone was on the bus even though two students were absent.*

pre·sump·tion (prĭ zŭmp′ shən) *n.* Something that is believed to be true without proof: *Our presumption that school would be canceled because of the snow turned out to be wrong.*

pro·ce·dure (prə sē′ jər) *n.* A particular way of doing something: *The surgeon followed the operating procedures very carefully.* **—pro·ce′ dur·al** *adj.*

prod (prŏd) *v.* **prod·ded, prod·ding, prods. 1.** To urge or stir to action: *I'm glad that my parents prodded me to take piano lessons.* **2.** To poke, jab, or push, as with a pointed object: *The shepherd prodded the sheep.*

pro·gres·sive (prə grĕs′ ĭv) *adj.* **1.** Continuing at a steady pace: *The progressive development of a new medicine requires constant work.* **2.** Moving forward: *The progressive storm is traveling across the country.* **—pro·gres′ sive·ly** *adv.*

pro·jec·tile (prə jĕk′ təl *or* prə jĕk′ tīl′) *n.* An object, such as a bullet, that is thrown, fired, or launched into space: *The projectile from the cannon destroyed the house.*

pro·jec·tion (prə **jĕk'** shən) *n.* Something that juts or sticks out: *Thorns are projections on rose bushes.*

prop·o·si·tion (prŏp' ə **zĭsh' **ən) *n.* A proposal, offer, or suggestion: *My sister made the proposition that she would do the dishes if I would sweep the floor.*

pros·per·i·ty (prŏ **spĕr'** ĭ tē) *n.* The state of having business success, wealth, or good fortune: *Many people have good jobs in times of prosperity.*

pro·tein (**prō'** tēn') *n.* A large group of organic chemical compounds that are the basis of all living cells and are the materials for cell growth and repair: *Including enough protein in the diet is important for healthy bodies.*

pro·voke (prə **vōk'**) *v.* **pro·voked, pro·vok·ing, pro·vokes. 1.** Cause; bring about: *The sad movie provoked tears from many in the audience.* **2.** To cause anger or irritation: *Taking away his toys provokes my little brother.* —**pro·vok'ing·ly** *adv.*

psy·chol·o·gy (sī **kŏl'** ə jē) *n., pl.* **psy·chol·o·gies.** The science that studies the mind, emotions, and behavior: *The psychology class helped teachers understand the behavior of their students.* —**psy·chol'o·gist** *n.*

R

rad·i·cal (**răd'** ĭ kəl) *adj.* **1.** Extreme: *Year-round school is no longer a radical idea.* **2.** Basic; fundamental: *In order to get into shape for soccer, I made a radical change in my exercise habits.* —**rad'i·cal·ly** *adv.* —**rad'i·cal·ness** *n.*

ran·dom (**răn'** dəm) *adj.* Not having a particular plan, purpose, objective, or pattern: *The random destruction from the tornado indicated that it skipped from place to place.* —**ran'dom·ness** *n.*

rash (răsh) *adj.* **rash·er, rash·est.** Acting with haste and recklessness: *It is rash to chase tornadoes.*

re·al·ism (**rē'** ə lĭz' əm) *n.* Presenting things as they really are in art, literature, movies, and television: *The movie was successful because its realism made people feel like they were there.* —**re'al·ist** *n.*

rear (rîr) *v.* **1.** To raise up: *The seal reared its head to catch the fish thrown by the zookeeper.* **2.** To rise on the hind legs: *When the horse reared, its rider fell off.*

re·bate (**rē'** bāt') *n.* A return of a sum of money that has been paid for something: *The rebate reduced the final price of the car by $1,000.*

re·but·tal (rĭ **bŭt'** l) *n.* **1.** The act of proving something false, especially by giving opposing arguments or evidence: *The debate team may give a rebuttal to prove the opposing team wrong.* **2.** A statement or argument that gives opposing arguments or evidence: *The defense attorney's rebuttal convinced the jury of the defendant's innocence.*

rec·om·pense (**rĕk'** əm pĕns') *n.* Payment for something done or given: *The recompense I received for the work was very fair.* —*v.* **rec·om·pensed, rec·om·pens·ing, rec·om·pens·es.** To pay for something done or given: *My sister and I are recompensed for doing yard work.*

re·deem (rĭ **dēm'**) *v.* **1.** To get back or recover: *The woman redeemed her diamond ring from the pawnshop.* **2.** To exchange or turn in for money or something else: *Mother redeemed her coupons for $2.00.* —**re·deem'a·ble** *adj.*

re·demp·tion (rĭ **dĕmp'** shən) *n.* The recovery of something given up or lost: *The redemption of my lost ring made me happy.*

re·dun·dant (rĭ **dŭn'** dənt) *adj.* Using more words than necessary; wordy: *The sentence could be shortened by eliminating the redundant words.* —**re·dun'dant·ly** *adv.*

re·frain (rĭ **frān'**) *n.* **1.** A verse or phrase in a song or poem repeated at regular intervals: *While one student read most of the poem, everyone joined in for the refrain.* **2.** The music that is the setting for this.

re·im·burse (rē' ĭm **bûrs'**) *v.* **re·im·bursed, re·im·burs·ing, re·im·burs·es.** To pay back: *Bernard reimbursed his sister for lunch.* —**re'im·burs'a·ble** *adj.* —**re'im·burse'ment** *n.*

re·ject (rĭ **jĕkt'**) *v.* **1.** To refuse to accept, believe, use, or go along with: *Teachers, parents, and students all rejected the plan to have school on Saturday.* **2.** To throw away or get rid of: *When I cleaned out my closet, I rejected the sweaters that no longer fit.*

re·lapse (rĭ **lăps'**) *n.* An act of slipping back into a former condition: *The patient returned to the hospital after a relapse.* —*v.* To slip back into a former condition: *During the winter I relapse into my old eating habits.*

rem·i·nisce (rĕm' ə **nĭs'**) *v.* **rem·i·nisced, rem·i·nisc·ing, rem·i·nisc·es.** To remember, tell, or write of past events or experiences: *My grandfather and uncle reminisce about their lives when they were young.*

re·miss (rĭ **mĭs'**) *adj.* Careless or neglectful in doing one's duty: *The guest was remiss in thanking the hostess as she left the party.* —**re·miss'ly** *adv.*

re·ne·go·ti·ate (rē' nĭ **gō'** shē āt') *v.* **re·ne·go·ti·at·ed, re·ne·go·ti·at·ing, re·ne·go·ti·ates.** To revise the terms of a contract: *When interest rates fell, we renegotiated the terms of our mortgage.* —**re'ne·go'ti·a·ble** *adj.* **re'ne·go'ti·a'tion** *n.*

ren·o·vate (**rĕn'** ə vāt') *v.* **ren·o·vat·ed, ren·o·vat·ing, ren·o·vates.** To restore to a previous condition or make as good as new: *The new owners renovated the old house before they moved in.* —**ren'o·va'tion** *n.* —**ren'o·va'tor** *n.*

re·pel (rĭ pĕl′) *v.* **re·pelled, re·pel·ling, re·pels.**
1. To drive off or keep away: *Some sprays repel mosquitoes.* 2. To cause dislike or disgust: *The candidate's dishonesty repelled the voters.* 3. To resist: *The raincoat repels water.*

rep·ri·mand (rĕp′rə mănd′) *v.* To scold severely or formally: *The principal reprimanded the students who deliberately tripped their classmates in the hallways.* —*n.* A severe or official scolding: *Sadie received a reprimand from her boss because she was constantly late for work.*

re·side (rĭ zīd′) *v.* **re·sid·ed, re·sid·ing, re·sides.** To live in or at a place permanently or for a long time: *The Malloys have resided on the farm for many years.* —**re·sid′er** *n.*

re·solve (rĭ zŏlv′) *v.* **re·solved, re·solv·ing, re·solves.** 1. To decide: *When I received a low grade I resolved to study harder.* 2. To solve: *My father was able to resolve my sisters' argument.*

re·vise (rĭ vīz′) *v.* **re·vised, re·vis·ing, re·vis·es.**
1. To read over, change, correct, and improve: *My teacher's feedback helped me revise my essay so that it was easier to understand.* 2. To change, make different, or alter: *The weather forecaster revised the forecast from rain to sleet.*

rhyme (rīm) *n.* 1. Words that end with the same or similar sounds: *The words "land" and "sand" rhyme.* 2. The similarity or repetition of sounds, usually at the ends of lines of poetry.

rit·u·al (rĭch′ōō əl) *n.* 1. A set form or system of ceremonial acts: *The rituals of the tribe are described in a book about its culture.* 2. A procedure or routine faithfully followed: *A walk is part of my daily exercise ritual.* —**rit′u·al·ly** *adv.*

ro·de·o (rō′dē ō′ *or* rō dā′ō) *n., pl.* **ro·de·os.** A show in which contestants show their skills in horseback riding, calf roping, and other events used in ranching: *Many local ranchers displayed their horseback riding skills at the county rodeo.*

rup·ture (rŭp′chər) *n.* 1. The act or process of breaking open or bursting: *The rupture of the blood vessel was serious.* 2. A break in friendly relations: *The misunderstanding caused a rupture in the girls' friendship.* —*v.* **rup·tured, rup·tur·ing, rup·tures.** To break open or burst: *The water main ruptured, so we were without water for three hours.*

S

sat·ire (săt′īr′) *n.* The use of humor or irony to ridicule or make fun of human faults or shortcomings: *The story is a satire of the desire to be rich.*

sat·u·rate (săch′ə rāt′) *v.* **sat·u·rat·ed, sat·u·rat·ing, sat·u·rates.** 1. To soak thoroughly to the point where no more can be absorbed: *The water from the broken water main saturated the surrounding area.* 2. To fill completely: *The smell of chlorine from the indoor pool saturated the gym.*

scar·ci·ty (skâr′sĭ tē) *n., pl.* **scar·ci·ties.** An insufficient amount: *The scarcity of medicine was a concern of the pioneers.*

sce·nar·i·o (sĭ nâr′ē ō′ *or* sĭ năr′ē ō′) *n., pl.* **sce·nar·i·os.** 1. An outline of a series of events: *The lawyer presented to the court a scenario of what happened.* 2. An outline of the plot of a play, movie, or story: *The movie producer liked the author's scenario for the movie.*

scheme (skēm) *n.* 1. A plan: *Iza developed a scheme to study for the test.* 2. A secret plan or plot: *The police uncovered a dishonest scheme to cheat people out of their money.* —*v.* To make or devise a plan. *Michael schemed to get out of doing his chores.*

scut·tle (skŭt′l) *v.* **scut·tled, scut·tling, scut·tles.**
1. To sink a ship by cutting or making holes in the bottom of it: *The enemy secretly tried to scuttle the ships.* 2. To abandon: *Because it rained, we scuttled our plans to go to the park.*

se·clud·ed (sĭ klōō′dĭd) *adj.* 1. Alone; shut off from others: *Many early settlers lived a secluded life.*
2. Hidden from view: *The children's hiding place was a secluded cave.* —**se·clud′ed·ness** *n.*

serf (sûrf) *n.* A member of a class of laborers owned by the landlord and bound to work the land. Serfs could not move off the land even if the landlord sold it. —**serf′dom** *n.*

ser·vi·tude (sûr′vĭ tōōd′ *or* sûr′vĭ tyōōd′) *n.* Slavery: *Servitude of others is not allowed in the United States.*

se·ver·i·ty (sə vĕr′ĭ tē) *n., pl.* **se·ver·i·ties.** 1. Seriousness: *The severity of the accident shocked the community.* 2. Harshness: *The lawyer said that the severity of the punishment did not match the crime.*

shoal (shōl) *n., pl.* **shoals.** A shallow place in a body of water: *The ship did not sail through the shoal.*

shrine (shrīn) *n.* 1. A place that is holy or highly respected for its history: *The people went to the shrine to worship.*

si·lo (sī′lō) *n., pl.* **si·los.** A tall building shaped like a cylinder that is used for storing food for livestock: *The farm animals will have enough food to eat this winter because the silo is full.*

sin·is·ter (sĭn′ĭ stər) *adj.* 1. Suggesting evil: *The villain's sinister look frightened the hero.* 2. Evil: *The sinister woman was convicted of murder.*

sloth·ful (slôth′fəl *or* slŏth′fəl *or* slōth′fəl) *adj.* Lazy; idle: *The rainy day made me feel slothful, so I just sat and stared out the window.*

so·ci·ol·o·gy (sō′sē ŏl′ə jē *or* sō′shē ŏl′ə jē) *n.* The scientific study of human social behavior and its history, organizations, and institutions: *Sociology helps us understand different cultures.*
—**so′ci·o·log′i·cal** *adj.* —**so′ci·ol′o·gist** *n.*

spend·thrift (spĕnd′thrĭft′) *n.* A person who spends money wastefully or foolishly: *The spendthrift spent a month's salary in just a few days,.*

sphere (sfîr) *n.* A round solid figure whose surface is the same distance from the center at all points; ball; globe: *The basketball trophy is a glass sphere.*

spoils (spoilz) *n.* **1.** The goods or property stolen or taken by force, especially in war: *The Vikings took the spoils of their conquests home with them.* **2.** The benefits gained by the winner, especially the winners of a political office: *The spoils the winning candidate received included an office computer.*

spright·ly (sprīt′lē) *adj.* **spright·li·er, spright·li·est.** Full of energy and spirit; lively: *My sprightly grandmother constantly thinks of things for us to do together.* —**spright′li·ness** *n.*

star·board (stär′bərd) *n.* The right side of a boat or ship as one faces forward: *We looked at the seals on the starboard.* —*adj.* Of, on, or relating to the right side of the boat as one faces forward.

starch (stärch) *n., pl.* **starch·es.** A food such as rice, corn, potatoes, and wheat that contains a nutrient that is made and stored in all green plants: *The menu included the starches rice and potatoes.*

stat·u·ette (stăch′ōō ĕt′) *n.* A small statue: *The statuette was so small that I could balance it on the palm of my hand.*

stern (stûrn) *n.* The rear part of a boat or ship: *There were seats in the stern of the boat.*

strad·dle (străd′l) *v.* **strad·dled, strad·dling, strad·dles.** To stand or sit with a leg on each side of: *When I first learned to ride, I found it awkward to straddle the horse.* —**strad′dler** *n.*

strait (strāt) *n.* A narrow passage of water or channel that connects two larger bodies of water: *Explorers hoped to find a strait between North America and South America.*

strat·a·gem (străt′ə jəm) *n.* A clever plan, trick, or scheme designed to gain a goal: *The hockey team members developed a strategem for winning.*

sub·ject (səb jĕkt′) *v.* **1.** To bring under control or authority of: *The dictator subjected the people he conquered.* **2.** To cause to undergo or experience: *The audience was subjected to a long boring speech.* —**sub·jec′tion** *n.*

sub·se·quent (sŭb′sĭ kwĕnt′) *adj.* Following or coming after: *When the ice storm downed power lines, subsequent efforts were made to restore electricity as quickly as possible.*

sub·sis·tence (səb sĭs′təns) *n.* **1.** The ability to survive or exist: *The subsistence of some species of insects has amazed scientists.* **2.** The means of support; livelihood: *The subsistence of animals depends on an adequate food supply.*

su·per·vise (sōō′pər vīz′) *v.* **su·per·vised, su·per·vis·ing, su·per·vis·es.** To watch over in order to oversee, direct, guide, or control: *The babysitter had to supervise the children on the playground to make sure they didn't get hurt.*

sup·por·tive (sə pôr′tĭv) *adj.* Giving approval, encouragement, or assistance: *The teachers in the school are supportive of their students' efforts to succeed.*

sur·mise (sər mīz′) *v.* **sur·mised, sur·mis·ing, sur·mis·es.** To think something to be true with little or no evidence; guess: *When the stray cat came to our door, we could only surmise as to how she got there.* —*n.* A guess.

sus·pend (sə spĕnd′) *v.* **1.** To stop or interrupt for a time: *After-school activities were suspended for a week because of bad weather.* **2.** To keep from attending for a while: *The students were suspended because they cheated on a test.*

T

tech·nol·o·gy (tĕk nŏl′ə jē) *n., pl.* **tech·nol·o·gies. 1.** The use of scientific knowledge and methods for practical or industrial purposes: *Astronauts use technology to study space.* **2.** The methods, materials, or objects used for practical purposes: *Computer technology has made communication faster.* —**tech·nol′o·gist** *n.*

ter·mi·nol·o·gy (tûr′mə nŏl′ə jē) *n., pl.* **ter·mi·nol·o·gies.** The terms or vocabulary used in a specific subject, science, art, or trade: *The average person may not understand the terminology of medicine.*

the·ol·o·gy (thē ŏl′ə jē) *n., pl.* **the·ol·o·gies.** The study of the nature and being of God and religious beliefs: *People may spend a lifetime studying the theology of their religion.*

thrift·y (thrĭf′tē) *adj.* **thrift·i·er, thrift·i·est.** Very careful with money and other resources: *The thrifty shopper always waited for sales before buying clothes.* —**thrift′i·ly** *adv.* —**thrift′i·ness** *n.*

tox·in (tŏk′sĭn) *n.* A poisonous substance produced by a plant, animal, or microorganism: *The scientists discovered a way to kill the toxin produced by the bacteria.*

tra·di·tion·al (trə dĭsh′ə nəl) *adj.* Of or relating to beliefs, customs, or knowledge that is commonly agreed upon: *The family wanted the traditional food that they have every year for Thanksgiving.* —**tra·di′tion·al·ly** *adv.*

tra·jec·to·ry (trə jĕk′tə rē) *n., pl.* **tra·jec·to·ries.** The path followed by something, such as a bullet, missile, or meteor, hurtling through space: *We use a telescope to follow the trajectory of the comet in the sky.*

tran·si·tion (trăn zĭsh′ ən *or* trăn sĭsh′ ən) *n.* The passing from one form, state, position, condition, or activity to another: *When the weather warmed, we made the transition from heavy coats to light jackets.* —**tran·si′tion·al** *adj.*

trem·or (trĕm′ ər) *n.* **1.** A shaking or vibrating movement, as of the earth: *The tremor caused by the earthquake made the dishes rattle.* **2.** An involuntary shaking or trembling of the muscles, body, or limbs: *Keith's illness caused a tremor in his hands.*

U

ul·ti·mate (ŭl′ tə mĭt) *adj.* **1.** Final: *The skater's ultimate goal is to win a gold medal in the Olympics.* **2.** Greatest possible: *Giving one's life to save another is the ultimate sacrifice.* —**ul′ti·mate·ly** *adv.*

un·ac·count·a·ble (ŭn′ ə koun′ tə bəl) *adj.* **1.** Unexplainable: *The suspect's whereabouts are unaccountable.* **2.** Not responsible: *The powerful man thought that he was unaccountable for his actions.* —**ac·count′a·bly** *adv.*

un·ac·cus·tomed (ŭn′ ə kŭs′ təmd) *adj.* Not used to: *We were unaccustomed to the heat of a July day in Tucson.*

un·am·big·u·ous (ŭn′ ăm bĭg′ yōō əs) *adj.* Unmistakable; clear: *I knew exactly what Ms. Leyden meant by her unambiguous answer to my question.* —**un′ am·big′u·ous·ly** *adv.*

un·bi·ased (ŭn bī′ əst) *adj.* Free of the tendency to favor one side or another; not prejudiced; fair: *The unbiased judge listened very carefully to both sides before making a decision.*

un·couth (ŭn kōōth′) *adj.* **1.** Lacking manners; crude: *The uncouth behavior of my friend embarrassed me.* **2.** Awkward; clumsy.

un·der·ling (ŭn′ dər lĭng) *n.* A person who is lower in rank or position than another person: *The queen ordered her underling to run errands.*

un·fath·om·a·ble (ŭn făth′ ə mə bəl) *adj.* **1.** Difficult or hard to understand: *The criminal's actions were unfathomable to his friends.* **2.** Very difficult or impossible to measure: *The size of space is unfathomable.*

un·flag·ging (ŭn flăg′ ing) *adj.* Untiring; not failing: *Fitz's unflagging efforts to write well paid off when his story won a contest.*

un·flap·pa·ble (ŭn flăp′ ə bəl) *adj.* Not easily excited, confused, or upset; calm: *The girl was happy that her parents were unflappable when she told them about her problem.* —**un·flap′ pa·bil′i·ty** *n.*

un·gain·ly (ŭn gān′ lē) *adj.* **un·gain·li·er, un·gain·li·est.** Awkward; clumsy: *The ungainly puppy had trouble running without tripping over his own feet.* —**un·gain′ li·ness** *n.*

un·pre·dict·a·ble (ŭn prĭ dĭk′ tə bəl) *adj.* Difficult or impossible to know or tell beforehand: *The election was so close that the final result was unpredictable.*

un·ru·ly (ŭn rōō′ lē) *adj.* **un·ru·li·er, un·ru·li·est.** Difficult or impossible to control, manage, or discipline: *The unruly child threw a tantrum whenever she did not get what she wanted.*

un·sa·vor·y (ŭn sā′ və rē) *adj.* **1.** Unpleasant, disagreeable, or distasteful: *I had the unsavory task of cleaning the fish.* **2.** Unpleasant to the taste or smell: *The room was filled with the unsavory smell of rotten eggs.* **3.** Morally bad or offensive: *The unsavory villain in the story caused problems for the other characters.*

un·sea·son·a·ble (ŭn sē′ zə nə bəl) *adj.* Happening or done out of season; not coming at the right or proper time or season: *The warm temperature is unseasonable for a January day in Missouri.*

un·wav·er·ing (ŭn wā′ vər ĭng) *adj.* Not changing or hesitating: *The soldier won a medal for unwavering bravery in battle.*

V

vague (vāg) *adj.* **vagu·er, vagu·est. 1.** Not clear in expression, thinking, or feeling: *The class didn't understand the teacher's vague explanation.* **2.** Not having a clear or definite shape or form: *The fog was so thick that the ship's outline was vague.* —**vague′ ly** *adv.* —**vague′ ness** *n.*

vent (vĕnt) *v.* **1.** To release or let out: *The worker vented the steam from the engine.* **2.** To express: *When the ice skater could not do the jump, she vented her frustration by crying.*

verse (vûrs) *n.* A part of a longer poem, song, hymn, or similar work: *Everyone had to memorize one verse of the long poem.*

ver·ti·cal (vûr′ tĭ kəl) *adj.* At a 90-degree angle to the horizon; upright: *Telephone posts are vertical to the ground.* —**ver′ti·cal·ly** *adv.*

vir·tue (vûr′ chōō) *n.* **1.** Moral goodness or excellence: *She is a woman known for her virtue.* **2.** A particular quality of moral goodness or excellence: *Kindness is a virtue.*

vi·sion·ar·y (vĭzh′ ə nĕr′ ē) *adj.* **1.** Characterized by an understanding of the importance of things before they occur: *Everyone was excited by the visionary plans of the school board.* **2.** Having impractical ideas or plans that exist only in the imagination: *The visionary predictions did not seem realistic.*

vi·sor (vī′ zər) *n.* The projecting brim on the front of a cap used to shade and protect the eyes: *The visor was a different color than the rest of the cap.*

vis·ta (vĭs′ tə) *n.* A view, especially a distant one seen through an opening or passage between buildings or trees: *The vista of the mountains and valleys could be seen from the airplane.*

vi·ta·min (vī′tə mĭn) *n.* Organic compounds needed in small amounts to stay healthy: *I like to know which vitamins are in the foods I eat.*

vo·lu·mi·nous (və lōō′mə nəs) *adj.* **1.** Having great size; large: *The voluminous stadium could seat 80,000 people.* **2.** Enough to fill or capable of filling a large volume or many volumes: *The class read the voluminous works of Shakespeare.*

W

wind·ward (wĭnd′wərd) *n.* The side or direction from which the wind blows: *To move to the windward.* —*adj.* On or moving toward the direction from which the wind blows. *Our cottage is on the windward side of the island.*

Y

yarn (yärn) *n.* A story that is often long and exaggerated: *The children listened to their grandfather's yarns.*

Z

zo·ol·o·gy (zō ŏl′ə jē) *n., pl.* **zo·ol·o·gies.** The science that studies animals and animal life: *Zoology helped me understand the life cycle of animals.* —**zo·ol′o·gist** *n.*

Standardized Test Practice

In lessons 1 to 36, you have concentrated on building vocabulary, a skill that is an important aid in reading comprehension. However, the competent reader must master a variety of other skills. These include the following:

- **Identifying main and subordinate ideas**—deciding what the most important idea in the selection is and what items support that idea

  Examples:
  Main idea   The ancient Maya had a fascinating culture.
  Subordinate   The ancient Maya developed irrigation.
  They created an accurate calendar.
  Mayan artists produced sculptures, painting, and jewelry.

- **Deciding on an appropriate title**—choosing a title that is closely related to the main idea of a selection

- **Drawing inferences**—coming to a conclusion that is not directly stated but is based on information given

  Example:
  If someone is breathing hard, you can infer that the person has been running.

- **Locating details**—scanning a selection to find the answer to a specific question

The following pages will give you a chance to practice the skills you use when you read. The questions they contain are the kinds of questions you will be asked to answer on a standardized test.

The reading selections include passages from science and social studies texts as well as informative essays and short narratives.

Reread the selection "The Pony Express" on page 15 and circle the letter of the BEST choice to complete each of the following statements.

1. Most people moved to the West after 1848 because
   A. they wanted adventure.
   B. the West had fertile farmland.
   C. the climate in the West was pleasant.
   D. gold had been discovered in California.

2. The Pony Express promised to deliver mail in
   A. a month.
   B. one week.
   C. three days.
   D. less than ten days.

3. The Pony Express was discontinued because
   A. too many messages had been lost.
   B. messages could be delivered faster by telegraph.
   C. bad weather made the journey on horseback too dangerous.
   D. Russell, Majors, and Waddell could not find enough riders.

4. The word *celebrated,* in line 34, means
   A. famous.
   B. had a party.
   C. old-fashioned.
   D. remembered a birthday.

5. The main idea of the selection is that
   A. Pony Express mail delivery was hazardous and difficult.
   B. Californians used the Pony Express to communicate with those in the East.
   C. the Pony Express surpassed stagecoach in rapid cross-country mail delivery.
   D. the craving for wealth prompted thousands of Americans to travel westward.

Reread the selection "Meteors" on page 29 and circle the letter of the BEST choice to complete each of the following statements.

1. Meteors can be seen

    A. once every ten years.

    B. during a solar eclipse.

    C. on almost any clear night.

    D. during certain seasons of the year.

2. Parts of large meteors, called meteorites, cause

    A. forest fires.

    B. temperature changes on Earth.

    C. an electromagnetic field to be set up.

    D. circular indentations in the Earth's crust.

3. From reading the article, you can infer that

    A. meteor showers are dangerous.

    B. scientists keep records of meteor showers.

    C. meteor showers occur at irregular intervals.

    D. ancient peoples believed that meteor showers brought good luck.

4. The word *heralded,* in line 21, means

    A. warned.

    B. produced

    C. introduced.

    D. announced.

5. The main idea of the selection is that

    A. meteors, debris drawn by gravity from comets, have landed on Earth.

    B. the largest recorded meteor shower occurred over North America in 1833.

    C. ancient people believed meteors to be omens of some approaching disaster.

    D. meteors leave depressions in the surface of the Earth when they collide with it.

Reread the selection "The Rescue of the Peregrine Falcon" on page 71 and circle the letter of the BEST choice to complete each of the following statements.

1. The word *gorge* as it is used in the selection means
   A. eat greedily.
   B. a steep-walled canyon.
   C. fashion a metal tool in fire.
   D. a wedge-shaped dress panel.

2. The following title would be a good choice for the selection on page 71:
   A. The Dangers of DDT
   B. What Peregrine Falcons Can Do
   C. How the Peregrine Falcon Survived
   D. The Decline of the Peregrine Falcon

3. Peregrine falcons began to disappear because
   A. they fought among themselves.
   B. they were overcome by their natural enemies.
   C. the climate in their habitat became much colder.
   D. their food contained high concentrations of pesticides.

4. The disappearance of peregrines in the 1940s could be described as
   A. unusual.
   B. expected.
   C. mysterious.
   D. frightening.

5. The reappearance of peregrine falcons was caused by
   A. a change in their feeding habits.
   B. the efforts of environmentalists.
   C. the development of stronger eggshells.
   D. the gradual adaptation of the birds to their environment.

Reread the selection "The Rocket's Red Glare" on page 155 and circle the letter of the BEST choice to complete each of the following statements.

1. A *catapult* may be described as

   A. a segmented insect.

   B. a fireworks element.

   C. a feline with a shiny coat.

   D. a device for launching missiles.

2. The following sentences summarize the contents of the first four paragraphs of the selection. The sentence that BEST summarizes paragraph 3 is the following:

   A. Rockets are based on Newton's Third Law.

   B. Europeans used rockets for both land and sea warfare.

   C. Germany launched rockets against England during World War II; today's rockets are fearsome weapons.

   D. The first step in the development of rocketry was the discovery that some materials can cause an explosion when they are ignited.

3. Europeans found that the equipment necessary for launching rockets was

   A. expensive.

   B. unavailable.

   C. heavy and bulky.

   D. overly complicated.

4. After rocketry was discovered, its FIRST use was

   A. in warfare.

   B. for fireworks.

   C. in construction.

   D. in transportation.

5. In nineteenth-century warfare, rockets proved to be more practical weapons at sea than on land because

   A. sailors were well trained in technology.

   B. rockets traveled farther on water than on land.

   C. there was more room on ships for the rocket launchers.

   D. the sails and tarred hulls of enemy ships were large targets.

Standardized Test Practice

Read the selection "Violent Vesuvius." Then answer the questions on page 191.

Violent Vesuvius

Kids Discover, August/September 1995

People who lived near Vesuvius in A.D. 79 thought of it as simply a very big hill. However, Vesuvius was really a sleeping volcano, silently and slowly building up pressure until it would one day explode.

On August 24, A.D. 79, after a series of small steam explosions made an opening at the top of the mountain, Vesuvius erupted. The blast shot pumice and ash toward the sky. After about half an hour, the pumice and ash rained down and began to blanket the city. The sleeping giant had awakened, with a deafening roar.

What caused Vesuvius to erupt? The earth's surface is made up of huge rocks, called plates. When the plates move apart or hit each other, molten (melted, liquid) rock, called magma, from deep within the earth is pushed to the surface by pressure from hot underground gases. The magma in Vesuvius was so hot and steam-filled that it turned to pumice. There was no lava in this eruption because the magma was too explosive and steam-filled to form lava.

Circle the letter of the BEST choice to complete each of the following statements.

1. Read the sentence below from the passage.

   The sleeping giant had awakened, with a deafening roar.

   In the sentence, the term *sleeping giant* refers to

   A. a volcano.

   B. the earth's plates.

   C. a person living near Vesuvius.

   D. a giant living on Mount Vesuvius.

2. Compared with the eruption of Vesuvius, a volcanic explosion that creates lava

   A. is not caused by molten rock.

   B. is less hot and contains less steam.

   C. has a smaller opening at the top of the mountain.

   D. does not involve the movement of the earth's plates.

3. Of the following phrases, the one that BEST describes magma is

   A. a steam explosion.

   B. extremely hot rock.

   C. a blanket of ash that covers a city.

   D. huge rocks that make up the earth's surface.

4. According to the article, what causes volcanoes to erupt is

   A. giants that live on top of mountains.

   B. dramatic changes in the ocean tides.

   C. rain clouds filled with pumice and ash.

   D. gases that force magma to the earth's surface.

5. The word *plates* as it is used in the selection refers to

   A. chinaware.

   B. the composition of the earth's surface.

   C. the place on which a batter stands in baseball.

   D. the representation of paintings and sculpture in an art book.

Read the selection. Then answer the questions that follow.

Gabria and the Storm

Gabria's mom was still at work when Gabria saw the lightning shoot wildly across the sky. Gabria loved to watch the rain, but when she heard a loud clap of thunder, she trembled. She went to the window to watch the storm approach. Gabria listened as the thunder boomed more and more often and the rain fell harder and harder. Her mom would not be home for at least an hour, maybe longer in this weather. Gabria began to worry about lightning striking her house. She picked up the phone to call her mom's office. "Hello, may I speak to Sue, please?" Gabria said to the receptionist. "This is her daughter."

"I'm sorry, Gabria, but your mom has left for the day," the receptionist replied. Gabria figured that her mom was on her way home. She got off the phone and started checking to make sure that all the windows were closed. As she walked around the house, she listened to the floor creaking and the wind blowing. The floorboards began to remind her of a person whining, and the wind began to sound like howling. In the kitchen, Gabria found an open window. The floor underneath it was soaked. She closed the window and went to look for a mop. She hoped that none of the windows in the house were leaking.

Just then Gabria remembered that her mother had noticed a crack at the bottom of one of the basement walls when they were playing table tennis last week. Gabria knew she should try to do something to keep the water from coming through the crack. If enough water got through the crack, the basement could flood. Gabria had an idea. She ran down the stairs to the basement and went straight for the shelves on the left-hand side. Her father had piled sandbags there. She thought that she could pile the sandbags up to the top of the crack. Perhaps this would stop the water from coming inside.

She looked at the crack. Water had just begun to seep through. One by one, Gabria carried the sandbags across the basement. She balanced them carefully until she had covered the crack. Then she sat back, stared at the pile of sandbags, and crossed her fingers.

No water was coming in. Gabria was relieved. Just then she heard her mother's car pulling into the driveway. Gabria got to the top of the stairs as her mother opened the front door. "Gabria, sweetheart! Are you okay?" Her mom dropped her bags and started heading down to the basement to check on the crack. "I thought you'd be swimming in here by now!"

"I'm fine, Mom," Gabria said, as she followed her mother to the basement. "Let me show you how I blocked the crack in the wall!"

Circle the letter of the BEST choice to answer each of the following questions.

1. Which of the following sentences BEST summarizes the passage?

    A. A young girl and her mother decide to have fun during a storm.

    B. A young girl who is home alone is frightened by thunder and lightning.

    C. A young girl who is home alone uses her good sense to solve a problem.

    D. A mother rushes home during a storm because she knows that her daughter is alone.

2. What did Gabria do after she remembered that there was a crack in one of the basement walls?

    A. She painted over the crack to seal it.

    B. She blocked the crack with sandbags.

    C. She called the fire department for help.

    D. She went to her neighbor's house to borrow a mop.

3. Which of the following words BEST describes Gabria?

    A. unsure

    B. friendly

    C. impatient

    D. responsible

4. Where does the action of the story take place?

    A. in Gabria's room

    B. in Gabria's house

    C. outside during a storm

    D. in the office of Gabria's mother

5. From the story, which of the following conclusions can you make about Gabria?

    A. She has a good memory.

    B. She looks like her mother.

    C. She lives in a small house.

    D. She likes to play in the rain.

Standardized Test Practice

Read the passage below and answer the questions that follow.

The Artist

Marie's father worked as a chef in the house of the great painter Pablo Perez. One day Marie went into the pantry to get some flour that her father needed. To her surprise, she found that she could hear everything Mr. Perez was saying through the thin walls. His words were as clear as a bell. He was teaching an art class in his studio, and Marie was fascinated by what she heard. She took the flour to her father and quickly returned to the pantry to listen.

Mr. Perez described how to use oil paints to create light and shadow, how to make objects appear closer or farther away, and how to make people seem cruel or pleasant. That night Marie lay awake thinking about all that Mr. Perez had said. She wanted to try painting too.

"Dad, may I get some oil paints?" Marie asked at breakfast the next morning.

Her father hesitated. "We can afford a few colors," he said, "but very few. And one brush. And some inexpensive canvas."

"But I want to really paint," said Marie. "How can I do that with just a few colors?"

Marie's father smiled. "You can make colors by mixing other colors," he said. "Wait and see."

That afternoon Marie's father purchased a few tubes of oil paint—blue, yellow, red, black, and white. Marie was amazed by the various shades she could create with just these paints. The following day she began "attending" art class in Mr. Perez's kitchen pantry. It wasn't easy to work in the small, poorly lit space, but she was determined. By late winter, she had a large collection of work. She might have continued her secret education through the spring had it not been for a moment's carelessness.

One day, listening through the wall, Marie heard a student grouse about not having the right shade of green to paint new spring grass. "Add some yellow," she said, right out loud. She clapped her hand over her mouth, but it was too late.

Immediately Mr. Perez was standing at the pantry door. "Why, Marie," he exclaimed in surprise, "what are you doing in here?"

"I'm having my art class," she replied shyly. She then explained how she had mixed her paints and listened in the pantry each afternoon.

Mr. Perez gazed around the pantry. "Come with me at once!" he ordered. He marched her into his studio. "Take a look at this magnificent use of color," he said to the startled students and held up the painting Marie had been working on. "This young lady has mixed all of these shades from just five tubes. She is an artist."

Marie was amazed. The great Mr. Perez was not punishing her; he was praising her!

From that day on, Marie attended art class in the studio. She was allowed to use a glorious number of paints. But she still mixed her own colors when she needed an unusual shade. After all, she was an artist.

Circle the letter of the BEST answer for each multiple-choice question.

1. Why did Marie first go into the pantry?
   A. to hide
   B. to paint
   C. to get flour
   D. to listen to a lesson

2. Which sentence is the BEST summary of this passage?
   A. A man does his best to help his daughter.
   B. A famous painter teaches oil painting in his studio.
   C. A girl learns to paint by making the most of what is available.
   D. A clever girl gets free art classes from a distinguished painter.

3. In this passage, which of the following happens LAST?
   A. Mr. Perez calls Marie an artist.
   B. Marie asks her father for paints.
   C. Marie attends classes in the studio.
   D. Mr. Perez finds Marie in the pantry.

4. What literary device is used in the sentence "His words were as clear as a bell"?
   A. simile
   B. metaphor
   C. onomatopoeia
   D. personification

5. Which of the following is a compound word?
   A. outer
   B. outcome
   C. freshness
   D. refreshed

Read the advertisement below and answer the questions that follow.

Fresh-Air Foundation Seeks Host Families

We are looking for families residing in rural areas to host city children for the summer. If you live in a rural area, please consider becoming a host family.

A Fresh-Air Foundation host family must

- live in a rural are
- have at least one family child in residence.
- agree to host the guest child for eight weeks.

A Fresh-Air Foundation host family must provide

- transportation for arrival and departure.
- telephone communication with the guest child's family.
- a private bedroom.
- three meals per day.
- access to emergency medical attention.

In addition, we hope that Fresh-Air Foundation Families will offer

- a summer of fun and adventure.
- a feeling of belonging.
- a taste of country living.
- a lifetime of wonderful memories.

Won't you share your summer with a child from Capital City? There are many children, aged 6 to 12, hoping to find host families, and we hope to place every one of them. The Fresh-Air Foundation staff will provide all of the information and support you'll need to have a wonderful summer.

To Apply

The first step to becoming a Fresh-Air Foundation family is to call (415) 555-0000 and request an application. Our office is open Monday through Friday, 10:00 A.M. to 5:00 P.M. Please return your application by April 2 so that we can complete our assignments by the earliest possible date. If your family is chosen, an information package about your summer guest child will arrive approximately two weeks before his or her arrival date.

Circle the letter of the BEST choice to answer each of the following questions.

1. What is the purpose of the advertisement?
   A. to inform people of the dangers of pollution
   B. to persuade people to allow city children to live in the country
   C. to inform people about the Fresh-Air Foundation and what it does
   D. to persuade people to make donations to the Fresh-Air Foundation

2. From the information in the advertisement, what can you conclude?
   A. The Fresh-Air Foundation is based in the country.
   B. Children from Capital City are all 6 to 12 years old.
   C. Children over 12 years of age cannot reside with a host family.
   D. Saturday is the best day to get in touch with someone at the Fresh-Air Foundation.

3. Which of the following magazines would most likely contain this advertisement?
   A. *Farm-Fresh Food*
   B. *Weekend Getaways*
   C. *Country Family Living*
   D. *Cars and Country Roads*

4. Which of the following statements is NOT a fact?
   A. Host families must have at least one child.
   B. Host families must provide access to medical care.
   C. Guest children will live with host families for eight weeks.
   D. All guest children will have a lifetime of wonderful memories.

5. When will a host family receive information about its guest child?
   A. on April 2
   B. two weeks before the child's arrival
   C. eight weeks before the child's arrival
   D. when the family calls the Fresh-Air Foundation

6. Which of the following qualities is the Fresh-Air Foundation looking for in a host family?
   A. wealth
   B. discipline
   C. friendliness
   D. intelligence

Read the selection. Then answer the questions that follow it.

Doctors Clean Up Their Act

1. Only 150 years ago, a doctor would do things that a six-year-old child today would know not to, such as to deliver a baby or perform an operation without washing his hands (perhaps right after caring for an extremely ill patient or handling a corpse). Thus, new mothers often died from a mysterious disease called "childbed fever." After surgery, a patient had only a 50 percent chance of surviving, even if the operation was successful.

2. Until the mid-1800s, most people believed that infections were brought on by evil spirits, poisonous gases called miasmas, or some other mysterious cause—terrifying because no one knew how to get rid of those things. Unfortunately for people who needed medical attention back then, doctors had never heard of germs.

3. Long before the nineteenth century, doctors and other educated people knew that there are living things too small to see with the naked eye. In 1674 Anton van Leeuwenhoek, an amateur scientist, discovered microbes—forms of life so tiny that they can be seen only with a microscope. Even so, it was almost two hundred years before anyone realized that some microbes can cause serious illness and even death.

4. In 1857 Louis Pasteur performed a series of experiments that showed that microbes are always present in the air and that they will grow when conditions are right. He also proved that diseases caused by microbes, such as anthrax, are easily spread.

5. At about the same time, Dr. Ignaz Semmelweiss was making a connection between harmful microbes and childbed fever. His work clearly showed that this often-fatal illness could be prevented if doctors would kill the germs on their hands before delivering a baby. Despite growing support for what was called the "germ theory of disease," doctors kept ignoring the evidence even though their patients were dying. They could not accept that the way they had always done things could be wrong.

6. Luckily, Joseph Lister read a paper written by Pasteur. It gave Lister an idea—to keep a surgical patient from dying of infection, keep germs from entering the wound. This idea, like Semmelweiss's, seems simple today, but it was revolutionary in 1865, when washing one's hands before touching a patient was difficult. There were few steady sources of hot water, hardly any indoor plumbing, and no antibacterial soap.

7. Despite those difficulties, Lister not only washed his hands before every operation; he also cleaned all surgical instruments with a germ killer called carbolic acid. In the hospital in Scotland where he was in charge of surgical patients, deaths from infection dropped dramatically. Like Semmelweiss, Lister encouraged others to use his antiseptic methods, but few doctors were willing to change their practices. Although he wrote about the success of his methods, he was largely ignored.

⁸ Lister did not give up. During the next ten years, he traveled, lecturing on the need to kill germs on surgeons' hands, on instruments, and in operating rooms. He demonstrated his methods in a large London hospital. Finally the medical community began to accept the relation of germs to infection and to see the value of antiseptic methods. Before he died, Lister's ideas were widely accepted. Thanks to Joseph Lister, millions who otherwise would have died from infection have recovered from operations.

⁹ The effects of Lister's work reach far beyond the operating room. Today we routinely scrub our countertops, throw away old food, and avoid drinking pond water. In great part because of Lister, we understand that something need not be visible to be harmful and that we must protect ourselves from these invisible enemies.

Circle the letter of the answer choice that correctly completes each statement.

1. This selection suggests that a child today knows more than a doctor in 1850 knew about
    A. doing experiments.
    B. using a microscope.
    C. performing surgery.
    D. the danger of germs.

2. The sentence from the selection that explains the "germ theory of disease" is
    A. "There were few steady sources of hot water, hardly any indoor plumbing, and no antibacterial soap."
    B. "Even so, it was almost two hundred years before anyone realized that some microbes can cause serious illness and even death."
    C. "Thanks to Joseph Lister, millions of people who otherwise would have died from infection have recovered from operations."
    D. "Long before the nineteenth century, doctors and other educated people knew that there are living things too small to see with the naked eye."

3. The main idea of paragraph 9 is that
    A. Lister's discoveries have affected everyday life.
    B. invisible life forms are both common and dangerous.
    C. fewer people die from infections today than in the past.
    D. people must take responsibility for protecting themselves.

4. In paragraph 7, the way the word *antiseptic* is used helps the reader understand that a septic wound is one that is

    A. surgical.
    B. infected.
    C. invisible.
    D. swollen.

5. The author suggests that doctors in the mid-1800s failed to change the way they did things because they were

    A. greedy for profit.
    B. coldhearted about suffering.
    C. ignorant about how the human body works.
    D. unwilling to consider new ideas about infection.

Word List

Word	Lesson	Word	Lesson	Word	Lesson
abundance	8	climate	17	enticing	4
accumulate	16	coarse	14	envoy	32
acquainted	10	collage	32	eruption	3
acute	11	commitment	27	escapade	26
additive	20	commotion	25	esteem	28
adequate	8	comprehend	25	evident	6
aggressor	28	concoct	19	evoke	28
agile	2	congruent	11	exaggeration	19
alliteration	35	considerable	7	excerpt	12
ambassador	10	consistent	1	exclude	12
ample	8	consume	30	exclusive	12
anonymous	28	consumption	30	excursion	12
antique	32	contention	22	expenditure	33
appendix	33	continent	17	exploits	1
application	34	contrary	22	extracurricular	12
approximate	4	convince	19	extradite	12
archaeology	21	corral	26	extraneous	12
aristocrat	23	correspond	4	extrasensory	12
aspect	28	corrupt	3	extravagant	12
assert	22	council	14	exultation	12
assortment	28	counsel	14	facet	22
attain	16	couplet	35	famine	13
audible	6	course	14	fiber	20
audition	6	craftsman	23	figment	1
auditorium	6	crave	4	financial	5
auditory	6	credit	5	forbearance	22
avalanche	32	criminology	21	foretell	25
ballad	35	culture	23	formally	14
ballast	29	cumbersome	34	formerly	14
ban	16	curfew	32	fracture	3
bankrupt	3	currency	5	fragile	3
barricade	32	cylindrical	11	fragment	3
becalmed	18	daunting	31	frail	3
befriend	18	dawdle	2	frugal	5
befuddle	18	debris	32	geology	21
bemoan	18	deceive	30	glacier	17
bloated	8	deception	30	gorge	16
booklet	24	decipher	13	gratify	16
bounteous	8	deficiency	8	habitat	16
bow	29	dejection	36	heed	16
brake	14	dependable	33	hemisphere	17
break	14	dependent	33	herald	7
brocade	26	depression	7	hieroglyphic	13
bronco	26	derisive	31	imagery	35
bustle	2	devise	7	impact	7
cabana	26	diligent	2	impose	22
calcium	20	discharge	34	inaugurate	4
calorie	20	dismiss	27	industrious	2
canal	17	dispute	31	infringe	3
capacity	25	disrupt	3	inject	36
cape	17	dominant	22	intermission	27
capsize	29	dynasty	13	interplanetary	7
cargo	26	economical	5	intersect	11
casserole	32	eject	36	isolated	19
catapult	34	emanate	7	isthmus	17
celestial	7	emperor	23	jettison	36
cholesterol	20	encounter	7	jocular	1
circulate	31	encroach	22	knot	29
circumference	11	endear	1	lariat	26
civilization	23	energetic	2	leaflet	24
clan	23	engulf	34	leeward	29

Word List 201

Word List

Word	Lesson
legendary	10
leverage	34
lineage	13
lumber	4
lure	4
lyric poem	35
makeshift	10
maladjusted	18
malcontent	18
malformed	18
malfunction	18
malnutrition	18
malpractice	18
manacle	27
manage	27
manicure	27
manual	27
manufacture	27
megabyte	24
megalith	24
megaphone	24
meter	35
microorganism	24
microwave	24
migrate	13
miser	5
missionary	27
motivate	31
narrative	10
nebulous	28
negligent	2
negligible	8
negotiate	19
nimble	2
nobility	23
novelette	24
objection	36
obtuse	11
onset	7
operetta	24
organic	20
overwhelming	4
parallel	11
parched	19
passport	33
peasant	23
pendulum	33
peninsula	17
pension	33
perceive	30
perception	30
perpendicular	11
personal	14
personnel	14
pesticide	16
physiology	21
platinum	26
ponder	25
porter	33
portray	1
poverty	5

Word	Lesson
practical	34
prairie	17
precarious	13
preservative	20
presume	30
presumption	30
procedure	32
prod	4
progressive	25
projectile	36
projection	36
proposition	31
prosperity	5
protein	20
provoke	28
psychology	21
radical	31
random	25
rash	10
realism	35
rear	19
rebate	9
rebuttal	9
recompense	9
redeem	30
redemption	30
redundant	9
refrain	9
reimburse	9
reject	36
relapse	9
reminisce	19
remiss	27
renegotiate	9
renovate	9
repel	9
reprimand	31
reside	4
resolve	19
revise	6
rhyme	35
ritual	13
rodeo	26
rupture	3
satire	35
saturate	8
scarcity	8
scenario	1
scheme	10
scuttle	29
secluded	22
serf	23
servitude	10
severity	25
shoals	29
shrine	13
silo	26
sinister	28
slothful	2
sociology	21
spendthrift	5

Word	Lesson
sphere	11
spoils	1
sprightly	2
starboard	29
starch	20
statuette	24
stern	29
straddle	19
strait	17
stratagem	31
subject	36
subsequent	25
subsistence	13
supervise	6
supportive	33
surmise	34
suspend	33
technology	21
terminology	21
theology	21
thrifty	5
toxin	16
traditional	10
trajectory	36
transition	34
tremor	25
ultimate	1
unaccountable	16
unaccustomed	15
unambiguous	22
unbiased	15
uncouth	15
underling	23
unfathomable	15
unflagging	1
unflappable	15
ungainly	15
unpredictable	15
unruly	15
unsavory	15
unseasonable	15
unwavering	31
vague	32
vent	34
verse	35
vertical	11
virtue	10
visionary	6
visor	6
vista	6
vitamin	20
voluminous	8
windward	29
yarn	28
zoology	21